F A M I

# FAMILY

*A Portrait of Gay
and Lesbian America*

## NANCY ANDREWS

HarperSanFrancisco
*A Division of* HarperCollins*Publishers*

FIRST EDITION

Library of Congress Cataloging-in-Publication Data
Andrews, Nancy, 1963–
    Family : a portrait of gay and lesbian America / Nancy Andrews.
      p.   cm.
    ISBN 0–06–250011–2 (alk. paper)
    1. Gays—United States—Pictorial works.
  2. Gays—United States—Family relationships—Pictorial works.
  I. Title
  HQ76.3.U5A53  1994
  305.9'0664—dc20                              93–37935
                                           CIP

94 95 96 97 98 ❖ WOR 10 9 8 7 6 5 4 3 2 1

# FOREWORD

*The family unit "is two or more persons who share resources, share responsibility for decisions, share values and goals, and have commitment to one another over time. The family is that climate that one 'comes home to' and it is this network of sharing and commitments that most accurately describes the family unit, regardless of blood, legal ties, adoption, or marriage."*

"The Definition of Family," from *A Force for Families*, pamphlet published by the American Home Economics Association

Like all human beings, gay men and women desire the comfort and love that "the family" ideally provides. We wish for our families to be a place of security, a refuge from the chaotic, threatening world around us. Yet, as homosexuals, we are likely to fear that if the families in which we were raised discover who we really are they'll no longer love us, that they'll banish us from home.

Sometimes we banish ourselves, fleeing what we fear our families will say or do. We move to distant cities, convincing ourselves that we're better off leaving our families behind.

It's ironic that some blame gay people for attempting to destroy the American family, when it's the prejudice and fear those people perpetuate that tears at our familial bonds. By reinforcing and repeating the hurtful myths about gay and lesbian life, they turn parent against child, child against parent, sister against brother, friend against friend.

Even when we don't flee our hometowns for the relative anonymity of the nation's urban areas, the fear of what our families might say or do silences many, keeping us from sharing our full lives with loved ones. We build emotional walls to protect ourselves, starving the life out of the relationships that could mean so much to us and those we love.

But we are not without family. Some of us have been lucky enough or have worked hard enough to remain a part of the families in which we were raised. Others have created their own families—their "chosen families"—in place of the ones they've lost or fled. And, as gay people, we are all part of that very large family of lesbians and gay men who yearn for a safe world in which we can live with pride and dignity.

It is this gloriously complex and diverse family that Nancy Andrews captures so magically in the images and words of her landmark portrait of lesbian and gay America. In *Family,* Nancy presents the real people and the lives obscured by the destructive antigay, "family values" rhetoric. We discover, not surprisingly, that behind the prejudice, hatred, and hardship, the lesbian and gay family is a varied and resilient lot.

The magic of Nancy's work is her apparent invisibility. Through these often arresting and emotionally charged portraits and oral histories, we see the people she wants us to meet and hear their voices as if there were nothing standing between us and them—no camera, no tape recorder, no photographer, no interviewer. Yet we know Nancy is there, wanting us to experience the joy, sadness, anger, courage, and pride that she saw and heard as she traveled the country meeting, photographing, and interviewing members of the lesbian and gay family. Luckily for us, we get to share with Nancy in that remarkable journey with the turn of every page.

ERIC MARCUS
*8 November 1993*

This is the book I looked for eight years ago when I began to realize that I was gay. I was in college, all my friends appeared straight, and my head was filled with only gay stereotypes. These stereotypes didn't fit my self-image, and I began to feel the need to learn more about myself and others like me. Gay men and lesbians were all around me, but with their chameleonlike quality, I didn't realize they were there.

Sometimes a photographer's work can be a picture of the photographer as well as of her subjects. When I talked with Jean Mills, working the Alabama land her father once farmed, I recalled my childhood on my family's farm in Caroline County, Virginia. Dan Stevens of Maine, who rattled on about his ancestors, reminded me of my late Aunt Margaret, who diligently traced our family back to Jamestown in 1619. When Allen Spencer talked of singing in his church choir, I thought back to my hometown Southern Baptist church, where my mother was the organist and I sang in the youth choir.

But even those whose lives bear scant resemblance to mine share a common thread: we are gay in a predominantly straight society. There are those who, if they could flip a switch and become straight, would gladly do so. Others, such as Ana Chang, are grateful for a gift that allowed them to see life a little differently, even at the expense of losing all contact with their parents.

Rejection by our families is often our greatest fear. If that rejection comes, gays turn to others like themselves to form a "family." (The word *family* is slang for "gay" in many parts of the country.) But, just as in any family, relations aren't always smooth. Some branches are embarrassed or enraged by others. Lipstick lesbians don't want gay women to be portrayed as bull dykes. Even the less than pious would excommunicate members of ACT UP who disrupt cathedral Mass. The burly boxer doesn't want to be associated with the drag queen. And the drag queen says individual freedom is what it's all about, *honey.*

As I searched for subjects, I operated under the assumption that I could find gay people anywhere; the only difficulty would be their willingness to be photographed. I wanted to show a reflection of America, from the politician to the Elvis impersonator. During my search a bar owner in Memphis flatly stated that there were no gay Elvis impersonators and that I needn't waste my time looking. But I found several.

I read hundreds of newspapers and newsletters, and questioned hundreds of people. When I asked about couples who had been together fifty years or more, many gays laughed at the mere possibility. But I found and photographed Gean Harwood and Bruhs Mero, who have been together for sixty-three years. Often I came across what I wasn't even looking for. Once, when I was searching for a Jewish family celebrating Sukkoth, a gay man, frustrated that he couldn't answer any of my queries, suggested that I might be interested in photographing Joseph Dittfeld—a Holocaust survivor.

Some lines repeated themselves throughout my journey. Whether it was Glenn Burke, growing up in sight of San Francisco, or Wanda Henson in Mississippi, many gay people recalled thinking that they were "the only one." Few interviews with men failed to lead to a discussion of AIDS, though lesbians who were interviewed seldom brought up the disease. The color red, symbolizing AIDS awareness, is omnipresent at gay events—whether a single feather in a New Orleans Mardi Gras ball costume or the ribbon on a cowboy's shirt in Arizona.

And though AIDS is woven into the fabric of our lives, it is too often used to define us as gay people. Once, at a showing of portraits of gays, three people from the audience complimented me on my "AIDS pictures." Yet I had not even mentioned the disease.

Nearly every person of color talked about racism; white people barely mentioned it. Charles Gervin, a black man who lives in Detroit, offered these words: "Yes, we talk about it as much among ourselves as we talk about it with you. As a white person with another white person, you might not be aware of how much racism impacts on you, but just as much as it impacts on my life, it impacts on your life." A black lesbian refused to be photographed because she said she would not let "some white woman" take her picture.

I found that much divides gay men and lesbians, for we are a reflection of society. But there is also a tremendous spirit of friendship and support. Strangers offered their homes, even when they declined to be photographed. This book could not have been completed without the generosity and hospitality of both gay and straight people across the country.

Often, photographers, driven to produce the most arresting pictures possible, portray gays only in extreme situations, and such photographs have been used to define gay people because of the lack of alternative material. That's why when a *Washington Post* colleague looked at my pictures, he commented, "But these people don't look gay."

The mere fact that the women and men in this book agreed to appear between its covers indicates that they are not typical lesbians and gay men. But it is my hope that their photographs and words provide a glimpse into the lives of all gay people.

NANCY ANDREWS
*August 1993*

## PHYLLIS HUNT AND TERRIE HARNER

*Phyllis Hunt, thirty-four, and Terrie Harner, thirty, have been together for three years. Terrie is a newspaper distributor and Phyllis is a cancer radiation specialist. They met through Excel, a program of Christian community living sponsored by the predominantly gay Universal Fellowship of Metropolitan Community Churches.*

*Phyllis and Terrie spend endless hours renovating their home in Arlington, Virginia. They were photographed in their dining room, which was decorated with a lace tablecloth, a brass chandelier, and taffeta curtains.*

*Phyllis:* I've always said this to Terrie, and I feel this in my heart. Next to Jesus, I love her first. Jesus Christ is my first love, and that's who I dedicate my being to. But next to Jesus Christ, I love Terrie the most.

I think that is really why we've made it. We have gone through some tumultuous times, but the reason we've been able to come out on the other side is because we both are grounded in a spiritual aspect of God, and for us that's Jesus Christ. And that's very important to me, and I think to Terrie.

It doesn't really matter if you're in a gay relationship or a straight relationship. Relationships take a lot of work and they take a lot of energy. And they take a lot of compromise.

*Terrie:* Well, it's equivalent to a heterosexual marriage, as far as I'm concerned. A marriage license is one thing, but I think the greatest vow that is taken is when we take our vows before our God.

*Phyllis:* And we've done that. I really believe that our relationship wasn't an accident. I feel like our relationship was "called."

RUTH ELLIS

*Ruth Ellis was born on July 23, 1899, in Springfield, Illinois. In 1937, she moved to Detroit to be with her girlfriend, Babe Franklin. They lived together for thirty-four years. Babe was a cook, and Ruth ran a print shop out of their house. Babe, eleven years Ruth's junior, died in 1975.*

*Ruth now lives alone in a thirteenth-floor apartment in a senior citizens building in downtown Detroit. She says people in the building wonder why she has so many young women friends, especially white friends. Ruth is a regular at the Detroit Women's Coffeehouse and at women's music festivals. At the coffeehouse she taps her feet to the music, and complains to her friends that the performing poet is using the pronoun* he *too frequently. "He, he, he. Why not she, she, she?" Ruth asks.*

*She was photographed in her apartment and in her living room on her exercise bicycle, a gift from some of her young lesbian friends.*

I guess I knew I was a lesbian in high school because I fell in love with my gym teacher. Now, she didn't know it though, but that was my love. I couldn't do anything, just admired her, that's all. All to myself. I didn't know anything about lesbian or gay people. I tried to find out what we did. I tried to hang around some sportin' women because I figured they would know, but they just laughed me off. They wouldn't tell me nothin'.

Springfield was a small town, and there wasn't very many places gay people could go. We went to a lady's house. She sold liquor. That was back when home brew was in style. I guess she was gay, must have been, but she had both men and women.

Soon after I moved to Detroit I met a couple of gay girls. Sometimes you can tell who's gay and who's not. They looked gay. I got acquainted with these girls, and they introduced me to more and more. Then after Babe and I bought a home, our house was the main place for gay people to come. Gay people didn't have anyplace else to go. Everybody would bring a bottle. We used to dance a lot. We had a piano in the basement, and we'd sing and play. We'd dance and drink and play cards.

Babe and I stayed together over thirty years, until the city bought our property and we had to move. That's when I moved into a senior citizens building. I wanted to come downtown, and Babe went out in the suburbs. We still kept in touch. That is where she passed, out there—in 1975, I think it was.

I didn't know anybody in this senior citizens building that was gay. Then this girl, she taught karate, she came and taught us adults how to take care of ourselves. I looked at her and I said, "Oh, I bet she's gay." After she left I wrote her a card and asked her if I could get better acquainted with her. She invited me over to another class, and I met a lot of the girls there. They were gay. They took me to one of these bars and I met the people there. The ball just kept rollin'. I kept meetin' the women, the women, the women, until, oh, I just know a gang of them now.

I am the oldest lesbian that they know of. That's it. Everyone wants to meet this old lesbian. They just take me around here, there, and yonder. I specialize in the women. I love women. Yes, lesbians, lesbians, lesbians. I get most of my joy from women. Since I met all these women, that's what's keepin' me alive.

THE SKINNER BROTHERS

*The Skinner brothers, once devout Mormons, are descended from a long line of Mormon pioneers. As children, Scot and Lee were deacons in the church. Lee, now twenty-nine, is studying for his master's degree in educational psychology while working at night providing care for elderly relatives. Dustin, nineteen, works at a fast food restaurant. Scot, thirty-one, writes features for the local paper.*
*The brothers live in Tucson, Arizona, and were photographed in Scot's house. They are, from left to right: Lee, Dustin, and Scot.*

*Lee:* I have always known I was different—always, always, always. It was never a choice, it was more a matter of how do I deal with it. I always knew Scot and Dustin were gay. Scot always had magazines of men, and I would steal them. I would hide them in my room, and then he would take them from my room and take them to his room. Back and forth. We both knew we liked these magazines, but we didn't talk about it.

*Dustin:* I didn't even know that Lee and Scot were gay. I knew I was gay before I knew they were, which was so stupid.

*Scot:* I didn't know Lee was gay until I saw him in a gay bar. And I thought Dustin was going to be straight. I was hoping that he would be straight—and praying. Not really, 'cause I don't pray. I really wanted him to be straight because at that time, two years ago, I just was very pessimistic. I thought life was just too hard for gay people. And I thought that, coming of age in a time of AIDS, he would have a much easier life if he were straight. I was hoping he would be straight, beyond whatever I may have thought about how my parents might have felt about having three gay sons. But I'm more optimistic now.

*Lee:* I just knew that was how it was gonna be, and I just hoped Dustin didn't have difficulty in dealing with it. But I didn't feel that he should be something that he's not.
Mother was super upset when she found out about Dustin, because he was her last hope. She kept holding out that he would be straight. Then when he was gay it really upset her. She cried and cried and cried. She said, "I understand he's gay and that's okay, but why are all my sons gay? Why couldn't I at least have one that could give me grandchildren?"

*Scot:* There is one thing that I will say that's very annoying about having two gay brothers. Well, there's nothing annoying about having a gay brother, but I can't tell you the number of idiots who have said to me, "Oh, have you ever fooled around?" It makes me really mad, and I just look at them: "No!" It's offensive for somebody to ask you if you fool around with your brother—and people ask me like it would be cool.
But the wonderful thing about just having gay brothers is that you don't have to hide anything. I can't imagine what it would be like to have a straight brother. I think it would be really interesting.

# THE PROM QUEEN

*Lorelei Holness, who was open about her sexual orientation in high school at the expense of taunts and being beaten up, never went to her senior prom. At the age of twenty-seven, she was crowned the queen of a very different prom, one for gays and lesbians of any age, the 1991 Prince William (Virginia) Gay and Lesbian Alliance Prom.*
*Lorelei and her date, Deborah Rowett, twenty-nine, were photographed at the dance. Lorelei is a student and banker. Deborah is a chemist. They live in New Jersey.*

*Lorelei:* It was the prom that I never went to in high school. Everyone got dressed up. You put on your dress, you do your makeup. And my lover dressed up in her tuxedo and bought me a corsage. It was exactly like a prom night—you get all dressed up and you're very excited: "Oh, wow, it's tonight." The energy was incredible, and other people too, they were that excited. This is our prom, the prom we never had. It felt like you were making up for time that was taken away from you. That night, when I was crowned I was on cloud nine. To me it was even more special, because at this prom I was allowed to be myself and I was with the woman I loved.

*Kate, forty-eight, and Seleta, sixty-two, have been together for eight years. Both women work the night shift. Kate is a medical technician. Seleta is a switchboard operator.*
*Both grew up in the Mississippi Delta, working on farms and picking cotton. Seleta is divorced. Kate has two children. They were photographed in the living room of their two-bedroom apartment in the South.*

*Seleta:* I've always been infatuated with women, even when I was real small. But, like anybody else, I guess you try and push this desire out of your life. But it stays with you. You can't get rid of it. I tried to suppress it, and I wouldn't talk about it. Then I decided to get married. I thought this would, I guess, cure my feelings. But after I stayed married for a while, it didn't. So then I just started doing some things on my own. We got divorced.

But all of my husband's family has always recognized me as one of the family. Not like the wife my husband has now, they don't like her.

Kate is actually my husband's cousin. One time I was visiting my mother-in-law, and I happened to run up on Kate and her lover over there. Kate wanted to talk to me then, but she couldn't. So, she got my phone number or I got her phone number or something. But it wasn't meant to be then. We were just in-laws.

Then after we started calling each other, she asked me if she could be a friend of mine. At first I said no. She wanted to be a personal friend of mine, and I told her no, because I was already in the family.

But then it went on and on, just as friends. It just kept on till it got to the point where I said yes, 'cause I realized that I had gotten a divorce and I was out of the family.

Don't anybody know about me and Kate. You know how older people are, they don't believe in that. They just think she's a roommate. She *is* a roommate, but that's as far as they know. And they love her to death.

*Kate:* I asked her out first. She was something that I just fell for. There was just something about her. I love her.

Seleta and I both work 11 P.M. to 7 A.M. We have breakfast every morning together. Then, we don't go to bed until the afternoon. We work together, we go shopping together, get groceries together, do all of that. It's fantastic.

# DAN STEVENS

*Dan Stevens is a ninth-generation Mainer. The youngest of five children, he lived the first forty of his forty-one years in his family home in Augusta. After caring for his elderly parents for the past several years, he moved into his own home.*

*Dan works as a paralegal and lobbyist, and serves as chairman of the Conservation Commission of Augusta and as vice chairman of the city's Historic Preservation Commission, and is a past president of the Maine Old Cemeteries Association.*

*He was photographed in his home in Augusta.*

Some branches of my family stretch back fifteen generations, including nine here in Maine. We've been in Augusta since 1780, and in Maine since 1650. My earliest ancestor, Thomas Morton, first arrived in Massachusetts in 1622. He was later sent back to England for putting up a maypole and dancing with Indians and providing them with rum. But he was able to return permanently in 1630.

If your family has been here and can be traced back any length of time, families tend to intermarry, since a lot of travel was not done at that time. There are several branches of the family, and the families married back and forth. It's a wonder we're not all idiots. Cousins married cousins, and genealogies become difficult. Many people would couple and have children, and wait for the minister to come around, since he wouldn't come around but every year or two. So they would get married and baptize their children at the same time, because there were no resident clergy to perform marriages.

We were brought up with a sense of family. Having lived in the same community for two hundred years, everyone knew who we were and we knew who everyone else was. It's a sense of who you are. This is your family, and this is what they have done. Not that you have to repeat it, but there is an expectation of who you are to be.

Being gay has always been a part of my life, especially with my family and friends.

# IN THE GAP

*In the Gap is a support group of two dozen gay, lesbian, bisexual, and transgender Asian and Pacific Islander youths aged twenty-five and under in the San Francisco Bay area.*
*Tho Vong, nineteen, is a dancer and a student at City College of San Francisco. Sean Nhan, twenty-one, just graduated from Stanford University and now works at an Asian community HIV project. Howard Kwong, twenty, is a student at City College and works as an administrative assistant at the Asian Business League.*
*Sean and Howard were photographed with other members of In the Gap at a cafe in the Castro District.*

*Tho:* Youth are not really well respected. So if you're young, other people just tell you what to do. They treat us like children. We call our group In the Gap because we don't have a place where we can be gay, Asian, and be youth. We can be in other organizations where you're young or you're gay and Asian, but never all three together.

*Sean:* In other groups, the issues that they talked about didn't really make any sense to me. I was just starting to come out, and my issues were different because I was still curious about what it means to be gay and what sexuality means, and in the older groups, those issues were already resolved. I was still dealing with family issues, and youth are still dependent on family.

I've met a lot of people through the Gap. But it's only one venue; it's a start.

*Howard:* People who are raised here in the U.S. are taught to think for themselves, and have their own opinions. Parents can't accept that. If we have our opinion and our parents or our elders have another, we are not supposed to follow our opinion; we're supposed to follow theirs. That's a clash right there. As teenagers or young adults in America, we have our own dress habits, we have our own culture. They can't understand that.

FRANCISCO MENDIVIL

*Francisco Mendivil was born in Mexico and spent most of his early childhood in a Mexican orphanage. When he was ten, an Arizona rancher brought Francisco to the United States to live and study English.*

*Now twenty, Francisco makes his living as a hotel waiter in Tucson, Arizona. He was photographed at one of his favorite spots in the desert near the city.*

I was born in Nogales, Sonora, Mexico, the youngest of four. I was raised in an orphanage for families that have kids they couldn't take care of. If the family had too many of them, you could put your kids there and the government took care of them.

There were about twenty of us. It was one huge, long house, all brick. The two main sides were all metal bunk beds. People would put sheets on the top, hanging down, so it would be like little houses.

This American guy would come down and take Christmas presents to kids every year, and he wanted to bring another kid up here. He'd already brought one, and he was like eighteen or so, and he wanted to bring another kid that was younger.

I really don't know why he picked me. I think it was because my family was willing to give me up. The other kids had a mother and a father and they didn't want to have their kids taken.

He brought me up here, with permission and all that, just to study the language. It wasn't like an adoption or anything. Spanish was my first language, then English was my second. I had to learn it because at home I was kind of put down. You know: "You stupid Mexican, you don't know English and you've got to know English. No Spanish here. This is not Mexico." I hated it but I learned it. I learned it really quick.

I hated myself—because I guess I wasn't what everybody else wanted me to be. "This is so lame, why can't I get a wife?" I thought, "There's something wrong with me." I always had hatred. I hated my family, for being brought up in an orphanage, being abused as a kid, being brought up to America, being left here alone, never them calling, never them visiting, never keeping in contact with me. The fact that my family said, "You can take our kid away from Mexico." I do feel like if I would have been brought up in Mexico, I would have been straight.

I hit high school and I ran away from home. I lived on the streets for a couple months till I made enough money to get a place to live. I worked seven days a week, day and night, busing tables.

I have always made it. I dropped out of high school, but I didn't stay in the streets. I don't regret leaving school, but now I'm going back to get my GED, just simply for the fact that it does matter when you go out for jobs. It looks better.

# PAUL HENNEFELD

*Paul Hennefeld has devoted an entire room of his Victorian house to his stamp collection. He has thousands of stamps and special-cancellation postcards that depict gay people or related issues.*

*In 1982 Paul, his partner, Blair O'Dell, and a handful of other collectors started the Gay and Lesbian History on Stamps Club and began publishing the* Lambda Philatelic Journal. *When the group applied for membership in the national stamp-collecting society the American Topical Association, their application was rejected. But two years later, after Paul began winning ATA awards with his gay collection, the club was granted membership.*

*Paul's collection consistently provokes reaction in an otherwise reserved environment. His stamps were turned away from one exhibition, and protested at another. But usually people read every word of Paul's exhibit text, and twice, tearful men have hugged the collector and thanked him for his display. Paul's collection received the ATA's second-highest honor—the Reserve Grand Award—at the group's annual show in 1987.*

*Paul, sixty, lives with Blair, forty-eight, his partner of eighteen years, in Montclair, New Jersey. He was photographed in his home holding a stamp of blues singer Ma Rainey issued by the nation of Gambia.*

I've always collected stamps, even when I was a boy.

I was collecting United States stamps when Jonathan Katz's book *Gay American History* came out in 1976. I was reading the book, and every time I came across someone who was on a stamp, it clicked. I said, "My God, there's a lot of gay people here on stamps. That would make a good collection." So that's what got me into doing a list for the collection.

I had had so much trouble accepting myself as a gay person. But if I had known when I was younger that all these people were gay or bisexual, I am sure I wouldn't have had such a difficult time. So I said, "This might be a good way of spreading gay history to the straight public and also gay public." So I've been outing people through stamp collecting before outing became the thing to do.

It's all on stamps. I have it beginning with Greek mythology and bring it right up to the present time. Because my collection is on exhibit I have to be very careful about the people I put in it. I wait for more books and documentation to back me up. People ask me how I know so-and-so is gay. I just say, "Well, I got it from these books."

There are several stamps with Martina Navratilova, my favorite. I even have some congressmen like Barney Frank because his signature is on the corner of each letter he writes, and that's called a franked envelope.

Jon Hinson is the only Republican congressman I have in the collection. He resigned from Congress in 1981 after he was arrested on a morals charge. After he gave up his seat they still used his envelope. But he wasn't a congressman anymore, so they stamped it from the clerk of the House of Representatives. They only used this for about a month after he left his job. That makes it quite rare—an unusual item.

# YVETTE'S FAMILY

*Yvette Gomez, nineteen, lives with her mother, Madeline Gutierrez; her two brothers, Manuel Gutierrez,*
*twenty-five, and Peter Gomez, twelve; and her lover, Mariya Sparks, twenty. The family's home is in*
*San Francisco's Mission District, on a street watched every night by the Guardian Angels.*
*Mariya and Yvette were photographed in their room; in Madeline's room when Mariya returned*
*home from a day's work (Mariya is standing); and making dinner with the family.*

*Yvette:* When I think of family, I think of cousins, uncles, sisters, aunts, and my grandmother. But as far as my immediate family, it's my mom, my brothers, my niece, and my girlfriend.

My mom suggested Mariya move in with us. Both of our mouths dropped open. I didn't expect my mother to be so open-minded. I was afraid to tell her that Mariya was my girlfriend. It's a shock when your straight parents ask your queer lover to move in. The whole family has it right under their nose, in their face every day. Mariya is the symbol of who I am. That is really bold. That's a lot for my mother to deal with.

My room wasn't big enough for the both of us, so we moved into the living room, which aside from my mother's room is the biggest room in the house. It's cool, with a nice view.

We rearranged everything, and realized, wow, this was going to be our space. Our room's got a lot of Mariya's stuff. Her presence is very visible; a lot of the walls are decorated and represent her, who she is, and her spirituality. The smell of the room is completely different. There are more scents, lotions, and certain oils and perfumes that are all Mariya's.

*Madeline:* I was in the kitchen one day, and Yvette just came in and said, "Ma, remember you said, no matter what we want, you'll always stand by us. Right?" I said, "Yeah, you're my kids, I'll always stand by you." I thought she was pregnant.

Then she said she was a lesbian. I said, "How do you know?"

What could I say, if that's what she wanted. I asked her if she was sure. She said yes. I said, "No, baby, you're not." I just put my head down and I started crying. And then she went and told Manuel, and then she said, "Do you still love me?" He said, "Yes, why not?"

I was just hurt and disappointed. I don't like to talk about it. I was disappointed because everything just fell apart. It doesn't hurt as much as it used to. It's fine; I'm not—on the inside. It's going to take me a long time. It's only been two years. My feelings are on and off, because she's my only daughter, and I wanted her to have kids. A mother's dreams are of her daughter's wedding.

Before, when I was by myself, I used to cry and say, "Why? What did I do?" Because I thought it was my fault. And then she said no. And I thought it was her father's fault, because her father was so mean—he's the one who changed her, made her do this. And she said, "No, it wasn't that, either."

I told my cousins, and I told my friends. I said, "If that's what she wants, don't put her down." My mom doesn't know. She hasn't told her. Her dad knows, but too bad if he can't accept it.

Peter didn't take it at first. He told her to get out. It was Yvette, Peter, and I at the table. Peter was sitting next to her, and she had told him, and he didn't say nothing. He put his head down, and then he started crying, which made me cry. And then he told her she had to get out. She just sat there. But he's accepted it now; he goes with her all over.

My thing is, I want her to be happy. At first, I was afraid she was going to get hurt out in the street, 'cause of all this fighting, and people are against lesbians and gays.

I didn't want her out in the street, and she would be out late at night with Mariya. I was worried. So I just told her, "Well, ask Mariya if she wants to come and stay with you. I don't care." But I didn't tell that it was because I didn't want her in the street, taking her home at night.

I told Yvette, "What's Mariya paying rent for there if she's always here? If you two are going to stay together, you might as well just work it out. If you can handle it, it's fine with me."

Yvette didn't believe me at first. It didn't bother me. Like I tell her: "What goes on behind your closed doors is your business. Just don't do it around Pete. I don't want you hugging her or kissing her around Pete. Or around Manuel"—because Manuel will not accept it either. I don't care, just as long as she doesn't do it around me or around my friends.

Whatever they want to do is fine with me, as long as they're not hurting themselves. I've accepted it; there's nothing else I can do. And I don't want to hurt her by saying, "You can't be here," because that's what you are. Take your children for what they are. Don't put them down. No reason to. You wouldn't get rid of them if they had some kind of disease, if they were deformed, unless you didn't have a heart. So why do it if they're gay or whatever?

*Mariya:* At first we had to be real cautious about how much time Yvette spent with me and how much time I spent with her family. And now we all spend time together.

When Yvette and I first discussed moving in, we said, "Okay, we're going to try it for a month," 'cause actually my living space where I was staying before was not working. But I was terrified. Because this is already established. And if Yvette decided she wanted to break up with me, I'd be on the street. But we made an agreement about that: she can't kick me out, because I pay rent.

I've never lived with anyone before, never lived with a lover. And that's scary. But I love it. I love going to bed with her and waking up in the morning wrapped around each other. I love dreading having to go to work together, and I love talking about what we're going to eat. Simple things. I hate doing laundry together.

JIM DEAN

*Jim Dean has worked in investments since 1987, and in 1992 he started a portfolio of gay-friendly companies called Dean's List.*
*Jim, forty-one, is divorced and has a ten-year-old son. He was photographed in the lobby of the Atlanta office of PaineWebber, where he is the only openly gay stockbroker.*

I have a couple of times had professional situations, shall we say, yanked out from under me because I was a gay man. People would call to have dinner with you, "Please bring a date," they would say. And you bring the date, and the next day all the deals are off.

I decided I wasn't going to have any more of that. I didn't have anything to be ashamed of, and I was going to look for an opportunity where being gay could be a part of my success rather than being an impediment to it. I had long been convinced that as gay and lesbian people, we have had a tendency to accept whatever professional services were there, and many times they were less than adequate. One area in which the gay and lesbian community was very ill-served was the investment services. No one was really making an effort to market to our community so that we could be investing with pride—and I'm talking about investing in companies with favorable policies toward gay men and lesbians.

I kicked the idea around. Is there a market, and can you offer a service that's of any value? It's one thing to pick a bunch of companies that treat gay men and lesbians well, but if they're poorly managed companies and they're a bad investment, I mean, what's the point in doing that?

So far, most of our investors have sent letters explaining to the companies that the stock was purchased because it was believed to be a good investment and because the company has an admirable record on issues of importance to gay men and lesbians. Recently, I got a letter from the chairman and CEO of a company to whom we addressed letters, and he's saving them. So once we send enough of them they will begin to have a tremendous influence. Every time we send one of these letters we reinforce a company that has already decided to do the right thing.

To people who boycott businesses that have homophobic practices, all I can say is "More power to you and I hope you succeed." But you've also got to have the carrot and the stick. What I'm trying to do is to encourage people who do have favorable policies and let them know that it's appreciated and back it up with investment money that might otherwise go elsewhere.

# ELIAS FARAJAJÉ-JONES

*Elias Farajajé-Jones, forty, an associate professor at Howard University Divinity School in Washington, D.C., is the school's only openly gay faculty member.*
*Elias lives with his sixteen-year-old son in Washington. He was photographed in his classroom, where he teaches The Sociology of Hetero-Patriarchy, Spiritualities in Color, and The History of the Early African Church.*

One of my cousins died. He had AIDS. I was asked to do the funeral, and my aunt said, "You know, of course, there's to be no mention of AIDS, there's to be no mention of him being gay." She didn't want to invite anybody, and it was all to take place in less than fifteen minutes at the grave site. People showed up anyway, and I said everything except the "A" word. I talked about how there's no such thing as shameful death; before it had been tuberculosis and then it was cancer, and now in our days we have something else.

As soon as it was over, my aunt came and threw herself on me: "I thought you were going to stand there in front of everybody and say it." She was so upset.

After that I said, "This is really ridiculous. I am going to put all my energy into dismantling this kind of behavior." I started thinking about focusing a whole course on HIV/AIDS. I knew that it was very risky because I would be really outing myself. Already my involvement with AIDS had been questioned by people in school. People would say, "Why is he so concerned about AIDS?" and "Why does he have so many friends that have AIDS?" and "Does he have AIDS?"

So I decided to go ahead and do it, and of course my colleagues went, "Oh my God, he's lost his mind. Why is he doing this?" Students were like, "Oh, God, we don't want to take this class and we don't want to talk about AIDS."

When they saw the books in the bookstore they were already shaken. When they came into the first class I told them, "Well, this is what we are going to do, and if you don't like it, I suggest that you leave right now."

# JEAN MILLS AND CAROL EICHELBERGER

*Jean Mills, thirty-one, lives on the family farm where she was raised in Tuscaloosa County, Alabama. Before she was tall enough to reach the pedals, she drove a pickup truck, helping her father feed the cows.*

*Jean and her partner of twelve years, Carol Eichelberger, forty-five, farm the land Jean's father cleared by hand with a mule. The two provide organically grown vegetables for the one hundred families in the Tuscaloosa County Community Supported Agriculture, a co-op the couple created four years ago.*

*Jean and Carol were photographed walking up their driveway at the end of a day's work, a flock of chickens in tow.*

*Carol:* Our first seven or eight years out here, we didn't interact with the community because we assumed that they weren't going to be pleased with us. It's really been the community coming to us.

*Jean:* When we were first out here together, we'd have people who would drive over just to see what was going on. We didn't like that very much, because I thought they were trying to figure out what these queers were doing up in the woods. So we sort of had a little bit of trouble at first making it clear that people couldn't just come when they wanted to. And I think that may have been something of a mistake.

We shunned them somewhat to start off with to draw a line that they couldn't still come on the property and go fishing when they wanted to, or coon hunting when they wanted to, or drop by and see how the land's doing. That was something people did. Just ride into people's pasture just to see what it looks like, to see if they got a bad case of green onions this year too, or how the crop was coming along.

But then with the gardening, we were more comfortable with people dropping by because we had something to talk to them about.

*Carol:* There's been a few old people Jean has had sort of a nodding relationship with. Whenever she sees them they're friendly, but she doesn't see them that often. But a few of them in the past years have come up here to ooh and aah over the garden. Jean may be living up here with this strange woman, but she is doing something that they recognize and value.

They'll come by and say, "Remember those collards you gave me last year? Well, you have any of 'em this year?" These old men, they always talk. They'll have garden talk. They'll want to know what we've got up.

Somebody who's not from this community doesn't get treated quite as well. There is a heterosexual couple that lives across the road; to us, they're very mainstream-seeming people. But, boy, everybody in the community has given them such a hard time, because they ride horses English style.

*Jean:* They put up a little pole to train on. Sometimes you go by and they are just riding in circles. It's just not real country behavior. People still just consider them weird. People probably think we are weird, but actually, our vegetable garden had legitimized us in a way.

THE DIGGING DYKES OF DECATUR

*With almost two dozen members, the Digging Dykes of Decatur work hard to uphold the proper garden club image. They consult eminent etiquette books from the early 1920s and read appropriate quotes at their monthly meetings, which are held in members' homes in this suburb of Atlanta.*
*"There's a sorority that one of us was a member of a long time ago," said founding member Janet Metzger. "Tri-Delt. And I thought 'DDD,' and we came up with Digging Dykes of Decatur."*
*Grand Czarina Sherry Siclair and other DDD members were photographed in Siclair's backyard, near her garden, which now lies dormant due to an accidental overdose of lime. Members in the background are Lisa Mount, Janet Metzger, Darlene Drury, and Laurie Kezh.*

*Sherry:* I used to call my mother during periods of depression or difficult times. One time when I was talking to her she said, "Well, honey, just keep a clean house."
I said, "Mother, I am keeping a clean house. And I'm still just miserable." And after a long period of time she said, "Well, I think what you need is to join a garden club."
And I said, "Well, Mom, I don't think that I would fit in too well." So she really studied on that, and then she said, "Well, honey, I think you should start one for your own kind."
So we did. I knew that you needed things like a quote for the day, and we needed a charm book. Our quote from the September meeting was: "A large bosom should be let alone with no attempt to hide it. Your legs are your friends, keep them together."

*Darlene:* There are no rules for membership. It's completely arbitrary.

*Sherry:* It's whoever can handle it.

*Darlene:* We had a member drop out and we asked her why, and she said, "Because you never talk about gardening."

*Sherry:* And she lied, because we talk about gardening at every meeting.

*Darlene:* That's right, two or three sentences. And the Grand Czarina said, "Well, you must never have been to a real garden-club meeting, then."
We were the biggest photo opportunity at the Gay Pride parade in 1990. A bunch of dykes in funny hats in a pickup truck with the Grand Czarina in her lawn chair with little twirly things that we attached to get attention.

*Lisa:* It proved, despite popular opinion, that lesbians do have a sense of humor.

*Laurie:* It's such a fallacy. The boys get all the credit for having the humor.

*Sherry:* As soon as we started it, the boys started flocking: "Can I join? Can I join?" Of course, you know we didn't allow the likes of them in here.

*Darlene:* It is the Digging *Dykes* of Decatur, thank you very much.

*Sherry:* And what would we call *them?* The Digging *Dicks* of Decatur? We said we'd certainly welcome an auxiliary. Someone that would make the pastries for the meetings, and clean up after the meetings, and do all those things. And you know, not a single one showed any interest in doing that.

ELVIS "THEMSELVIS"

*America has a passion for Elvis Presley that surpasses all boundaries. Two lesbians, miles from each
other, have a common bond with Elvis: they both impersonate the King.*

*At the age of twelve, Leigh Crow cried in bed at summer camp when it was announced over the loud-
speaker that Elvis had died. She would never get to see him play. Now, at twenty-seven, Leigh has her
own band, Elvis Herselvis, which plays to both gay and straight audiences.*

*Polly Wilmoth, forty-eight, also cried when she heard that Elvis was dead. She and her lover of nine-
teen years, Linda Reynolds, live together in Florence, Mississippi. Polly is a truck driver.*

*Polly was photographed in her front yard; Leigh in her bedroom in San Francisco.*

*Polly:* I have a Graceland Mobile Home. It's got everything in it but a built-in guitar
Jacuzzi. Come out of Alabama, special picked, ordered off the line just like you would
have a car chosen for a certain style.

Elvis was my idol. Even when I was a kid, listening to him on the radio just tore me down.
Growing up, I got a cigar box and a stick and put me some rubber bands on it. Then when
I got to be about fourteen, I started playing the guitar.

We got a lot in common. He's from Mississippi. I'm from Mississippi. He loved his mother.
I love my mother. I came up poor like Elvis. I drive a truck, been a twenty-four-year veteran on the highway: "sit on a concrete seat" is what we mainly say. And he drove a
truck.

Don't nobody look like Elvis. I just like to dance, and I've got the Elvis way of dancing. But I don't ever consider I'd ever be Elvis. Never will. I just think that somehow or another I can just, I can feel his soul when I'm movin'.

When he died, it came over on the truck's radio and I just fell across the wheel cryin'. I didn't go to work the next day. "Elvis is dead." I just got tired of hearing it—but the spirit hangs with me.

*Leigh:* Halloween of 1989, this girl I was going out with and I were going to be Elly May and Jethro from *The Beverly Hillbillies.* But then we got in a fight, so I didn't know what to wear. So I thought I'd be Elvis. I wore a blue sharkskin suit, wool and silk blend, real fifties, shiny; a pink shirt, skinny blue tie, white shoes, pink socks, and the hair.

My first show was for a friend promoting a weekly women's club. She had a lesbian performance every week. We were saying what we really needed was a drag show, because the other stuff would get heavy a lot of times, and stand-up comedy didn't really go over. So we were trying to figure out stuff that would lighten up the tone. I had just dyed my hair black. And I was teasing her, doing my Elvis impersonation. So she said, "You can do an Elvis drag."

"Oh no I can't," I said. I just didn't think that a bunch of politically correct San Francisco dykes were going to go for Elvis drag. But they got really silly. I started doing it all over town, lip-syncing. I knew the songs really well. I had sung along with the record for so long already that it only took some practice in front of the mirror to really get it down. Plus with Elvis you have this leeway: as long as I was curling my lip, it didn't matter that I wasn't right on the words.

# CHRIS RUSH

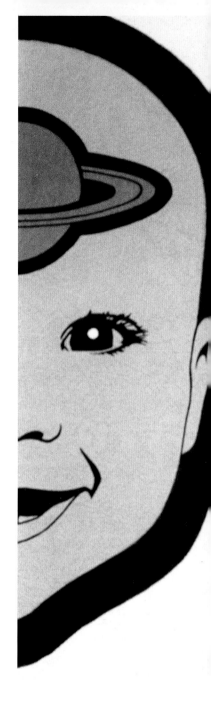

*Chris Rush, thirty-seven, lives with his lover of nine years, Victor Lodato, twenty-seven, in Tucson, Arizona. Chris spent ten years in New York City as a jewelry designer, once creating a diamond-and-emerald rosary for Imelda Marcos.*
*Chris still pays his bills by designing jewelry, but he is known around Tucson for his mural art. Though he paints in brilliant colors, Chris is color-blind. He was photographed in front of Baby Saturn King, which he painted on the side of an abandoned topless bar along Speedway Boulevard in Tucson. The mural survived for three months, until bulldozers destroyed the building.*

I couldn't work anymore in the land of millimeter. I needed to do work that was very bold and immediate. I started out doing street art. My work would appear and disappear in all different parts of the city. I started out putting work just wherever it suited me, but then I realized it wasn't fair to the struggling merchants of the world. So now I only put my art on derelict buildings or spaces I have permission to use. People are relieved to see the artwork on buildings that are kind of sad. It's a relief to see these buildings come back to life, even just for a second, because I have put artwork on them.

There's a really big difference between art that is for pedestrians and art that you would see when you are driving by. Tucson is a big car town. I wanted to do work that was big enough and placed right so people would see it when they drove by. I figured when people aren't watching TV, they are driving in their cars, and they are already in a bad mood because they are going to work. Somehow it makes it a little more fun for them.

The reason I paint babies is that they are this crazy race that lives among us. They are uncivilized, totally selfish. They're creatures of the id. They do whatever they want to, but somehow they manage to make us all think they are really cute.

I can have babies act out anything, and people will adore them. It's somewhat ironic as a queer that I have chosen babies as my means to get into the system. I am never gonna have them. And babies are the personification of all that family-value foolishness. But I just turned it back in their face, because I was a baby once. I was a darling baby once.

The way the gay experience has been defined for males of my generation is that the artists must document the apocalypse—they are the truth sayers. But I am interested in another side of the world, another part of my life. I don't want to do work that is always black and red and depressing. I am trying to do work that really celebrates how wet, wild, and green life really is. If you're gay you're supposed to be so burdened, and I just feel my sexuality is completely funny and ridiculous.

*Michael Petrelis, thirty-three, likes to point out that he was "raised by heterosexuals" in New Jersey. Now, as a full-time protester for ACT UP (AIDS Coalition to Unleash Power) and Queer Nation, he travels widely, from dogging presidential candidates on the campaign trail to attending a military trial in Japan for the murder of a gay U.S. sailor.*

*Michael was part of the much publicized protest in New York's St. Patrick's Cathedral that disrupted Mass in December 1989. More than one hundred people were arrested, including Michael, who stood on a pew blowing a whistle and screaming, "O'Connor, you're a murderer," at Cardinal John O'Connor.*

*Michael, armed with a fax machine and an ability to attract media attention, has been seen on every television network and in many newspapers across the country. His family is supportive of his activism, with his mother asking only, "Why don't you smile?"*

*He was photographed outside the ACT UP offices in Washington, D.C.*

A lot of my rage comes from seeing friends dying. The government's indifference. The drug companies charging too much money. I've got to say that a lot of my anger also comes from the apathy of the gay community, which by and large thinks that the government is doing enough to find a cure. You can't have conflict resolution without the conflict. And I'm just one of those people who is abrasive, is adversarial, and thinks that's the mentality we ought to have in our political approach.

In the late seventies I was living in group houses, and I remember this one guy Billy, who died of what is now called AIDS. But at the time he had these mysterious diseases. There was this disease going around that men I had slept with were dying of. Mel in New York had the same symptoms as this roommate in San Francisco: the diarrhea that wouldn't go away, the fevers that never came down. I've seen friends dying since the late seventies, and I can't really say that we have made a lot of progress in the fight against AIDS.

I was diagnosed as having Kaposi's sarcoma, which is a cancer that scientists generally believed to be related to AIDS. So I had all of these tests done. Then the doctor said, "Well, you've got AIDS. Go to GMHC"—that's the Gay Men's Health Crisis—"and get registered for Social Security benefits, draw up a will. There's nothing that we can give you." They didn't even have AZT at the time. It was August 26, 1985.

That was the demarcation line. I would just go to these meetings and scream at politicians that they weren't doing enough about AIDS and that they needed to do more. Everyone in the political circles really hated what I was doing. I just didn't let up in terms of screaming at people, and eventually I hooked up with some other angry gay people and we formed the Lavender Hill Mob. It always made me more angry that other gay people would say, "Don't scream at a politician. Trust us. We're quietly and nicely talking to these people. We're making progress." And I'm still seeing hundreds of people dying.

# SUSAN HESTER

*Susan Hester, forty-two, was with her partner, Mary-Helen Mautner, for nine years. Mary-Helen died two and a half years ago of breast cancer. She was an appellate lawyer at the Department of Labor.*

*Susan works full-time as the director of a cancer project named for Mary-Helen. The Mautner Project provides support for lesbians with cancer, and works to increase the awareness of women's cancer issues.*

*Susan was photographed in her bedroom while she looked through an album made up of letters friends had written about Mary-Helen for their daughter, Jesse. They live in Washington, D.C.*

Mary-Helen wanted a child, and I had never thought about it. At first I wasn't particularly interested. But Mary-Helen was very committed; she was the one who explored all the possibilities.

We decided to adopt. She went through the adoption process. Almost no one knew which of us adopted Jesse. We didn't want anybody to act like one of us was more her mother than the other. So we got Jesse in 1984, when she was sixteen days old.

When Jesse was a year and a half old, Mary-Helen had a recurrence of cancer, which was a surprise to us because we had been told that she was in this very good category for not having a recurrence.

It changed our lives. It was a constant presence, but Mary-Helen was really determined: "I'm not a person with breast cancer." She didn't want it to be her identity.

Three weeks before she died, Mary-Helen was in the hospital. I had left the hospital for a short while to go get Jesse, and when I got back Mary-Helen looked totally different. She was just radiant, and she said, "I've had this idea."

While she was having a bone scan she had thought about how she was there by herself, but that I was coming back. She thought of all the lesbians who could be in the hospital with nobody coming back—no partner, no support person. She said, "We have to start a project." She had written down a page of notes.

The Mautner Project was her idea, and I think we've done good justice to it. I couldn't be prouder. It's provided a way to help other people who are going through what we did. The project has been really, really good for me. It has been a healing peace for me, having

gone through it with Mary-Helen. But on the other hand, I'm conflicted about it. I'm resistant to being so identified and associated with cancer, because it's horrible.

It's being constantly confronted with the disease and with people dying. It's so painful, so awful. It's a personal struggle for me, figuring out how much longer I am going to do this. How much more of my identity do I want it to be? It's a hundred percent now. It couldn't be more.

So who do I do it for? I don't think I do it for Mary-Helen. I do it for me. I do it for the other women. But I miss something about Mary-Helen every day. That doesn't change.

BRENDA CRAWFORD

*Brenda Crawford, forty-six, is an organizational development consultant in Oakland, California. A self-proclaimed groupie, Brenda helped form the People of Color Gay and Lesbian Alcoholics Anonymous Meeting and founded the African American Lesbian Fear Group and the African American Lesbian 40+ Group.*
*She was photographed on the balcony of her penthouse apartment.*

I came out when I finally met another lesbian. Her name was Mina. I had never seen a woman like Mina. She had this butch haircut. She had on this man's shirt and these men's pants and these men's shoes. I was fascinated by her. She took me into this club, and it was just like being in heaven. The women were dancing with each other, and the men were dancing with each other, and I was like, "I have arrived." I can still see that picture. I was just walking around, smiling, looking at people. I had known that I was gay since I was fourteen years old, but I hadn't had anyone to talk to about it. Here I was, seventeen, and this woman, in one night, opens up the world for me.

These women were from what we call the "old school." The butches had on the men's clothes, and the femmes had on dresses. I didn't really know where I fit in that whole scheme of things. I had on a pair of pants, and I did notice that I was attracted to the women with the dresses.

After that evening was over, Mina said to me, "I will come and pick you up tomorrow, and then you and I will go talk." So Mina came and got me the next day, and she proceeded to give me the proper protocol in terms of lesbian lifestyle—butch and femme protocol. She said, "People tolerated you last night because they knew you were new. But you never go up and ask a woman to dance who's sitting beside another woman, unless you ask the butch can you dance with her woman. And also, you don't smile at everybody, either."

I was a baby-doll butch, a teddy-bear butch. I had a little short haircut. I looked like a little boy—as my mother puts it, *tomboy.* I just think that's a lesbian in training. But I never fit the kind of image of the butch that Mina had in mind.

During that time, lesbians had these artificial families that we created. Mina must have been thirty, and she called me her son, and her woman was my mother, and I'd have sisters and brothers who were other members of the lesbian community. We would go to these bars, and we would hang out.

In terms of that kind of acceptance, it was really pretty wonderful, but in terms of the rigid kind of requirements that were laid upon me, I didn't fit that. Those roles are not as pervasive as they once were, but there are still women who very much are into that. There was a denial about those roles, and there were people who said those roles were negative, and that they were not empowering, were not affirming of lesbian lifestyle, that they were oppressive.

But I don't see it as all negative. In terms of my acceptance in the lesbian community when I came out, it was a very warm process because of the kind of structure that was there.

*"Lavender cowboys" is how the tour guide in San Francisco describes certain nineteenth-century residents. They seem to have congregated in the city and danced together at the bars.*

*Today, the descendants of those legendary cowboys ride a different sort of range, following the rodeo circuit—both gay and straight—around the country.*

*"It's in my blood. Horse fever," said Gene Mikulenka, thirty-five, of Houston, Texas, a champion pole racer. "Once you get it into your blood, it never goes out."*

*The first official gay rodeo was held in Reno, Nevada, in 1976. The reigning emperor of the drag imperial court held a rodeo to raise money for muscular dystrophy. The rodeo became an annual event, growing from a handful of contestants to several hundred, and drawing thousands of spectators. By 1983, state and regional rodeo associations had begun forming, and in 1993 there were fifteen rodeos on the circuit.*

*At first glance, there seems to be very little difference between a straight rodeo and a gay one. There's the dust and dirt, and the same pungent smells associated with livestock. Contestants follow the western dress code of Wrangler jeans, pressed long-sleeve shirts, and white cowboy hats.*

Image is important to contestants. "There really are gay people that can present themselves as a cowboy or cowgirl and not a bunch of sissies or drag queens," said Dan Iversen, thirty-eight, former president of the Arizona Gay Rodeo Association. Contestants like to point out that their rides are just as tough as those in a straight rodeo: a two-thousand-pound bull doesn't lose any weight when it comes to a gay rodeo. A gay rodeo tests the same ranch-hand skills that a straight rodeo does: casting a rope to catch an errant steer, breaking a wild horse, or speeding your horse past the herd on the range. Many of the events remain the same—bull and bronco riding, calf roping, and barrel racing. But there are also the crowd-pleasing "camp events" such as steer decorating, with the sometimes messy job of tying a ribbon to the animal's tail.

Both weekend cowboys and professionals compete on the gay circuit. "Unfortunately, in the straight rodeo, we can't let them know that we're gay," Gene said. But it is not all bad, according to Gene: "A lot of those guys at the rodeos are Christian, and they don't judge you." But, he adds, "I don't flaunt it."

Andy Anaya, twenty-eight, from Tucson, Arizona, earns his living by team roping, going to three or four rodeos a week. "When I first started going to the gay rodeos," Andy said, "I felt out of place. And now it's turned around. When I go to a straight rodeo I feel like I'm out of place."

These photographs were taken at the Atlantic States Rodeo in Upper Marlboro, Maryland, and at the Saguaro Regional Rodeo in Tucson, Arizona.

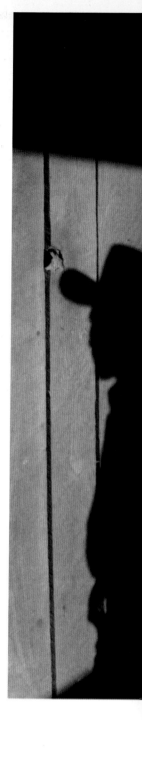

## T. J. SMITH

*T. J. Smith grew up on a farm in southeast Oklahoma. He started rodeoing at the age of ten and has worked with horses all his life. He is a quarter-horse trainer, farm manager, and coach for champion amateur and junior riders.*
*He is forty-three and lives in Edmund, Oklahoma. He was photographed in the stalls at the Atlantic States Rodeo.*

Well, you can't judge a book by looking at its cover, and I am gay. And I will be gay if it means life or death. I won't deny it. The only reason that I would deny it would be if it would make it better for everyone concerned. But I cannot see a point that would make it better for everyone concerned. I am who I am.

When I started going to the gay rodeos I felt, here's something that's among my peers, with people that are just like me, people that have gone through most of the same things as me.

It helped me accept myself. It was just a void in my life, and I really didn't know this is what it was. But it fills a void in my life. I just felt like I was freed. I feel like a bird that was in a cage that was turned free. And I think it will carry on through the rest of my life. Now, you know, if I die tomorrow, I'd feel like I'd had a complete life.

# DENNIS TERRELL

*Dennis Terrell, twenty-nine, the son of a ranch hand, grew up near Canton, Texas. He started rodeo-*
*ing when he was "a little bitty feller—probably five or six, maybe. I rode sheep in the peewee rodeo."*
*In college, Dennis rode bulls for Sam Houston State University in Texas. He lives in Tucson and*
*makes his living as a team roper with Andy Anaya on the rodeo circuit.*
*The photo showing Dennis standing in the center was taken at the Atlantic States Rodeo. Others pic-*
*tured are, left to right, Andy Anaya, Greg Olson, Larry Jones, and to the right of Dennis, David*
*Stinson, T. J. Smith, and Dan Iversen. Bull rider Cheryl Pollock is held in front.*

I love to rodeo. I get to rope with my best friend in the whole world. I get to travel all over
the country looking at beautiful country with my horse and doing something that I love.
Andy and I had never really known any gay people that were cowboys. Finding the gay
rodeos was really neat because, here we are in our element, making our living with our
horses, around gay people. It's a first for us. It's like a godsend.
When I was young you'd hear people talk: "Well, it's normal for little boys to do things." I
guess I was about twenty-two when I was really like, "Look, I'm stuck with it. I didn't ask
for it. But I might as well make the best of a bad situation."
It was something I was really always scared of, and it was like, taboo. If you're gay, you're
bad seed. So you just kind of went and secretly made out with somebody and then you
grabbed your laundry and you were gone. You didn't want to talk to 'em because you
thought it was bad. It took a lot of time to finally get over that.
Now, oh God, I wouldn't be any other way. It's what I am, and I've learned that it's not a
bad thing. It can't be against God's will, because I know for one I didn't ask for it. I was
born this way. I know I was. I mean, love is love. Whether you love a man or you love a
woman, that's what the world is missing a lot of—just love.
To me, the fun isn't the straight rodeos, because we just go to those, do what we need to
do. The trail on pro is so grueling: you are up one day, and you get in the truck and you're
gone to the next one because you're entered in one tomorrow.
There's a few guys at the straight rodeos that suspect, but they don't know. They respect
us because when Andy and I go to rodeos, we're real professional. We go and we can beat
them. I think that most of all they hate to say, "Oo-whee, those queens just beat us." They
respect us for our talent mostly.
This is my profession. I spent a lot of time getting good at it. You find your niche, your
knack, and you grind it, and grind it and grind it, every day. Just like anybody would go to
school and work at being a good lawyer or a doctor. I want people to take me seriously.
When I'm out there in the arena I hope they'll enjoy it, first of all, but I want them to
know that "he's good and he works at it." We work at it hard.

CANDY BELL

*Candy Bell, thirty-four, is a bull rider on the women's professional circuit. Her father was a bronco rider. She is also a safety engineer for the Gila River Indian Reservation in Arizona. She and her partner, Jodi Hines, live in Maricopa. Candy was photographed after completing her ride at the Saguaro Rodeo.*

The animal is worth fifty points and the rider is worth fifty points, for a possible one hundred points. So if you've got an animal that's not doing much, then you spur to try to get him to buck more.

I rode steers for a year in the gay rodeo. Then in Wichita, Kansas, I had what they call a little bunny hopper, a real straight bucker, and you have to spur a lot in order to score points. I got off the steer and went over to Jodi and said, "I am bored." So I thought I'd ride bulls.

Bull riding—90 percent of it's mental, being able to keep your focus. I have a spot on the animal where I focus—on its neck. They say wherever you look, that's where you're gonna go, so if you concentrate on keeping your focus on that spot on the neck, then you're going to stay right there, square with the animal. If you lose your focus and look to the side, then that's probably where you are going to end up.

My goal when I ride is not to conquer the animal but to be as one with the animal. I just want to stay with this animal for the amount of time, and to not be fighting against him. For me it's like being able to climb on an eagle's back and get up there and see the world as he sees it.

# GLORIA JOHNS

*Gloria Johns, a mental health counselor, lives and works on her native Gila River Indian Reservation in Arizona. She is a member of the Pima tribe. Gloria, fifty-two, has a partner and a ten-year-old son. She was photographed on the reservation.*

Once I worked in the alcohol and drug-abuse program. The staff there had their turquoise, and their long hair, and a lot of Indian stuff. And I thought, "Where's my Indian stuff? Where's my jewelry? What is going on?"

And the more I looked, the more I felt, "Gee, where's my Indianness? Is there something wrong with me?" But that's the only time I've questioned myself, who I was. And then later on I said, "Gee, I'm okay. I don't have to advertise it. I'm Indian."

The more I thought about it, the more I felt I'm Indian. And I guess the more I begin to work with the alcoholics, the program, the treatment, and stuff, I realize they've lost themselves somewhere in the process of their drinking. And that all they had is this debris inside. They don't know what's inside anymore. And they have to sift through that and clean it up and find out who they are, to be able to say, "I'm proud to be Indian."

# AVERY'S FAMILY

*Three-month-old Avery has two mothers, a father, and a long, hyphenated last name. The family is represented by fictional names. Laurel, thirty, and Peter, thirty-one, are doctors. Margaret, thirty-three, is a systems analyst.*

*The two women have been together for five years. They asked Peter, a gay friend, to father the child. Laurel is the biological mother. She used Peter's sperm, which he donated in her name at a local sperm bank.*

*The child lives with Laurel and Margaret. Peter visits her almost every day. He sent out 120 birth announcements after Avery's arrival and regularly carries around an Avery photo album. Peter was photographed holding Avery at the women's home in the South.*

*Laurel:* In the beginning we went back and forth. We had concerns . . . if we use a known donor and one day he says, "I'm gonna take this kid." What about an unknown donor? How do kids feel if they don't know half the biological? Sperm donors fill out a questionnaire, but how do you know that's accurate? It seemed so impersonal, sort of like picking shoes: "I'd like the brown ones with the laces." I wanted to know more about the donor's personality.

We were trying to think of what's the best thing to do. What if you have a kid that wants to know the father later in life? So that's where Peter came in. The first scenario was with Peter as donor, but no involvement with the baby.

*Peter:* I said no. I couldn't do it and walk away. It would have been like, "Here's the sperm, good-bye." I said I'd want to be a part of any person I had helped create. I'd want them to know who I was. I have my need to have children and my desire to have children. I couldn't do it and walk away.

*Margaret:* I think it got down to the matter of family and that the father's identity would have been a big secret to try to keep. So we decided to have a known donor.

*Peter:* It took me about a month to say yes. I wanted to see research about gay parents and how their children feel. Everything said the children would turn out just as well as any other average kid. I didn't want this to be selfish, to bring a kid into the world. Then we each had our lawyers set up the donor agreement, which was designed to work if we have a falling-out.

*Margaret:* The donor agreement let you know where the other person was coming from. It helped me know where I was too.

*Peter:* It was stressful—negotiating a deal. But it's something I never thought would happen. You don't hear of gay men having children. I always wanted kids. That was the one thing frustrating me about being gay. I'm an only child. I have no cousins. I'm the end of the line. My mother feels gay parents should have their kids taken away from them. It's unfortunate, because it's the only grandchild she'll ever have.

*Laurel:* Our family is just like anybody else's family. Just the fact there are two moms and a dad doesn't change the fact that it is a family. It just may not be the typical family.

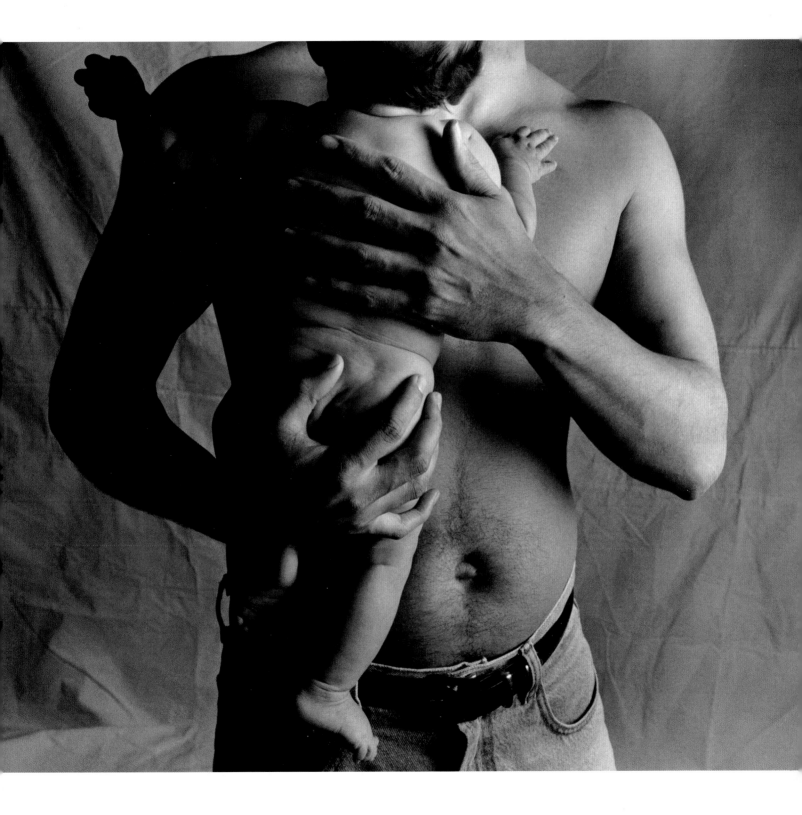

*Lenora Trussell, forty-two, Kathy Kigin, twenty-nine, and Sam Trussell, five, live in a turn-of-the-century white frame house in Colonial Beach, Virginia. Kathy and Lenora have been together for four years. Former city dwellers who moved to the country in search of a calmer life, Kathy and Lenora run a bed and breakfast in the rural town along the Potomac River. Lenora also works as a nurse and a masseuse, while Kathy stays at home and takes care of the family.*

*Sam refers to both women as "Mom," using their first names when confusion arises. The family was photographed in their front yard while Sam hugged Big Bird, his pet chicken, and his two mothers watched from the porch.*

*Lenora:* Sam defines a lot of our relationship. We met just after he was born.

Kathy called me up and said that she'd like to come over and talk with me about having a baby, because she was thinking about having one. So she came over, and she was totally Barbara Walters all day. She asked me every question under the sun. We talked all day long, so at the end of the day she said, "I would really like to spend more time with children, and I'd love to spend more time with a lesbian's child. How would you feel if I came over, like on Saturdays, and hung out with Sam for a few hours?"

I said, "Oh God, I'd love it. That would be wonderful." And so she did.

*Kathy:* Then all of the sudden, it was the same old story: every Saturday, I went to Lenora and Sam's and spent the day with them. But then things started to shift a little bit. I remember it. It was that hot summer weather sinking in.

*Lenora:* We actually said that we would never live together. We were going to buy two mobile homes and live next door to each other. Now that we have a mortgage together, I'm a lot more secure. It's funny what a little piece of paper will do. I do say we're married, but I quit saying it in front of Sam after he freaked out. That was just awful.

*Kathy:* He went to school and said something and came back spouting, "Two women can't get married."

*Lenora:* He said, "That's really sick," for two women to get married. I went crazy. Unfortunately, he doesn't have any other children of gay people he can be around.

*Kathy:* He always tells people that he has two mamas.

*Lenora:* At this point, because he doesn't really understand, he doesn't talk about us being lesbians. He doesn't say a word to anyone, but he hears it all the time.

*Kathy:* He hears *dyke, faggot.*

*Lenora:* And *gay,* and *homosexual,* and . . .

*Kathy:* He's never repeated a single one of those words.

*Lenora:* Not that we've heard him say. We don't know what he says. He could be having a conversation with his buddies and his buddies are saying, "We're Presbyterians," and he'll say, "Well, my mothers are lesbians."

# NELITA WILLIAMS AND BARBARA HUDSON

*New Orleans natives Barbara Hudson and Nelita Williams met on Mardi Gras Day seven years ago. Although both women say they knew they were gay at a very early age, both have been married. Barbara was married for twelve years and has two children. Nelita was married for twenty years and has six children. Just as the last of their children were reaching adulthood, Barbara, forty-nine, and Nelita, forty-eight, faced parenthood again when Nelita's five grandchildren unexpectedly moved in with them.*

*Nelita is a secretary, and Barbara cares for the children. Nelita, her youngest son, Barbara, and the five grandchildren live in New Orleans. The family was photographed on their front porch. In the photograph from left to right, back row: Quinton, Kiana, Nelita Williams, Barbara Hudson. Front row: Breana, twins Nelita and Redius.*

*Nelita:* My son in Alaska got in trouble. He is now in jail. He had five children, and their mother was not able to care for them. The children were placed in foster homes. The social worker there called me and said my son wanted the children with me.

Well, I'd rather them be here with me than be placed in different homes, since they couldn't be with their own mother and father.

But since he and their mother were not married, Louisiana doesn't consider them to be my grandchildren. We had to go through a lot of red tape. I found out the children were in foster care in February, and I didn't get them until October.

I had never seen the children before. We had to meet them about midnight at the airport, and our close circle of lesbian friends went with us. They also helped get beds, clothes, baby cribs, a playpen, and a walker. Different couples have told us that if we wanted some time to ourselves they would keep them. We haven't taken anybody up on it.

So we're parents all over again. It's something we weren't expecting, having to start over again at this age. We can't just get up and go, or sleep late. We can't do any of this anymore.

*Barbara:* That's the hardest thing, and we're still going through it. I get up every day at about quarter after six and bring Nel to work while her son is still here, before he goes to school. By the time I get back, some children are up. We get up and have breakfast, get dressed, wash two loads of clothes almost every day—a white and a colored. Then it's lunchtime. At about 2 P.M. we have a snack; then I'm back in the kitchen preparing supper. So my day is basically spent in the kitchen and running behind children.

*Nelita:* We're happy. We have a good relationship. We don't know what it's going to lead to with the children, but we're going to try our best to make them happy and keep them together.

*Jo Deutsch, thirty-two, Teresa Williams, thirty-five, and Jacob Deutsch Williams, two, live in Wash-*
*ington, D.C. Jo, a lobbyist, and Teresa, a massage therapist, have been together for eight years.*
*Jo, Jacob, and Teresa were photographed at Jacob's birthday party in their home.*

*Teresa:* We want Jacob to know right from the start that he is not alone, that there are other kids that have parents like his parents. For him that is the norm. He knows more kids who have gay parents than kids who have straight parents.

*Jo:* The birthday party was all the people that Jacob has known since he was born and the community that we've made here. It is a community of other gay and lesbian parents, Jacob's play groups, and people we've met socializing together. Sooner or later, when he goes to school, the entire circle of kids that he is going to be with are going to be kids who have either a single parent or straight parents. So it is important for us that he knows he's not the only one like this in the world. Right now he probably has absolutely no idea that he is in the minority.

*Teresa:* It's been a very reflective time, looking back at the birthday and the birth. After having gone through the birthing experience, there's something really special, something really sacred. Though I am not a religious person, there's a deeper knowledge of what's involved in us all being here. And there's a specialness to life and to the way we acknowledge being here on birthdays that I didn't have before.

*Jo:* There's such an amazing sense of pride. To think back on his first birthday, when he sat outside not understanding why all these people were around. Then to switch to birthday number two, where he understood *birthday* and he understood presents.

It's fun to watch him blow out a candle, when a year before we put the cake in front of him and he didn't even know to eat it. Next year he'll be lighting the candles and blowing them out over and over.

# STEVE FONG

*Steve Fong, twenty-five, is the secretary of the San Francisco Log Cabin Club, a gay Republican group in a city that is only 17 percent registered Republican. He has worked on campaigns, going door to door. During one election he registered Democrats as Republican voters in an effort to defeat an anti-gay politician in the primary.*

*Steve was photographed in his apartment in the Haight Ashbury section of San Francisco. He works as a security guard.*

I've been a registered Republican since I became eligible to vote. On a national level I really had a problem with the way the Democratic party operates as far as the special interests go. I found it very, very hard to be moderate and pragmatic because everybody had their own little extreme. Not that I disagree with them all the time. A lot of times I agreed with them, but I hate the polarization. I was trying to find my own sense of belonging, and the libertarian wing of the Republican party made it easy. It doesn't matter as long as you live your life well and you mind your own business. I'm much more pragmatic and moderate in my views than most people, especially in San Francisco. I identify more with Republicans.

In San Francisco, there's not much sympathy for Republicans. My friends are all mostly Democrats. Some of them make fun of me in a very, very nice way. I haven't really encountered anybody who really is so fanatical about it that they can't take it.

# THE CONGRESSMEN

*There are only two openly gay members of Congress—Barney Frank and Gerry Studds, both Democrats from Massachusetts.*

*Barney, fifty-three, was first elected to Congress in 1980. He and his partner of five years, Herb Moses, thirty-six, live together in Washington, D.C., and also spend time together at their home in Massachusetts's Fourth Congressional District. Barney is an attorney. Herb is a mortgage banker.*

*Gerry, who learned to speak Portuguese in order to help his election prospects in the fishing town of New Bedford, has been in office since 1972. Gerry has a partner of three years, Dean Hara, thirty-six. Dean works in association management. Gerry is a former schoolteacher.*

*The two congressmen were photographed in the rotunda of the House of Representatives' Cannon Office Building.*

*Barney:* I am doing everything I can in both my public life and my personal life to demonstrate to the majority of Americans how unfair and unjustified anti–gay and lesbian prejudice is.

I recognize that for many gay and lesbian people in the country, especially in areas where their own legislators are unfriendly, Gerry Studds and I are seen as a source of help. Unfortunately, both my staff and my own time are limited, and when it comes to individuals, I have to give the highest priority to the people who live in my district. In egregious cases, where an anti–gay or lesbian action against a particular individual somewhere else in the country indicates that there is a fundamental policy that needs to be changed, I do get deeply involved. For instance, when the Federal Emergency Management Agency under President Bush began actively persecuting a gay man, including efforts to force him to divulge the names of other gay and lesbian people in the agency, I invoked the powers of the subcommittee I chaired to force them to back down, and we succeeded in reversing that policy. In this case, we were helping an individual but we were also helping establish a fairer policy for the entire country.

*Gerry:* We really have two constituencies, but the important thing always to keep in mind is that the first and paramount one is the one for whom we work and in whose name we serve here. And I figured out very early on in this situation that the best way I could be of whatever help I can to the national constituency that I inherited ten years ago is to be the best damn congressman I could possibly be for my 1/435th of the country. If I tried any

other role, like being "the gay congressman," I would have done them an enormous dis-
service by being promptly defeated first term.

Bear in mind that there was a while here when there were so few women that they themselves, and some of them still do, have a national constituency. The same thing is true of
people of color, Hispanic Americans—although there certainly are more of them, obvi-
ously, than openly gay members at this point. There was a time when they assumed a
role, by default, of a national constituency as well as local.

# DALE MCCORMICK

*Dale McCormick, forty-six, was among the first females to become a journeyman carpenter. She has written two books on carpentry and founded a statewide nonprofit organization, Women Unlimited, which trains women in trade and technical jobs. In 1990, Dale was elected Maine's first and only openly lesbian state senator.*

*She and her partner, Betsy, live in Monmouth. Dale was photographed in the basement of her home, which she is in the process of building.*

I wanted to make a difference. My decision to run was the slow eradication of many barriers, both internally and externally created. If you went back to my high school annual, it says, "Dale will be the first *lady* vice-president of the United States." Which I think is telling—one, because they had to say "lady" because of the time; and, secondly, they couldn't have me be the president because of course that would have been too much for the time.

When I realized I was a lesbian, which happened maybe two or three years later when I was nineteen, I thought all that was not possible for me. I thought many things were not possible for me. It took maybe twenty years to slowly get that back.

When the *Webster* decision came down from the Supreme Court and the issue of reproductive choice was thrown back to the states, I began to realize that my internalized homophobia was a petty reluctance and that I—living in the Senate district of the ten-year incumbent, right-wing point man for the Christian Civic League—that it would make a difference if he wasn't there and I was there instead.

I won the election, though my opponent gay-baited me from day one, continually brought it up. I had death threats on the phone machine. I felt very vulnerable that whole time. It's like being naked in a glass house—just very hard emotionally that way. There was always this negative outpouring of energy from the right-wingers in the district and the fundamentalists. They wrote letters to the editor about Satan and Sodom and Gomorrah and "insult to womanhood." But that created a much greater reaction from the forces of light in the district, who wrote in saying wonderful things.

In my next election my next opponent, having learned from that, decided to be very nice. My opponent didn't raise the gay issue at all. It dropped off from being an issue almost immediately upon my election. It was hardly ever mentioned. It just went away to the point where I even forgot about it. I really think running for office is great therapy for getting rid of internalized homophobia.

I basically have periods of time when I forget that I am a lesbian. I hardly have ever in my life, ever, lived like that. I don't mean forget as in *ignore,* but to forget as in "be just as good as everybody else." And just as entitled to all the things everybody else is entitled to. It's a self-esteem thing.

I think that's what internalized homophobia is: you self-select yourself out of things because you think they are closed to you—relationships with children, personal conversations, or touching someone when you think that might be misconstrued. It's constantly being aware of who you are rather than reacting purely from your center. I think that's true for everyone.

CLEVE JONES

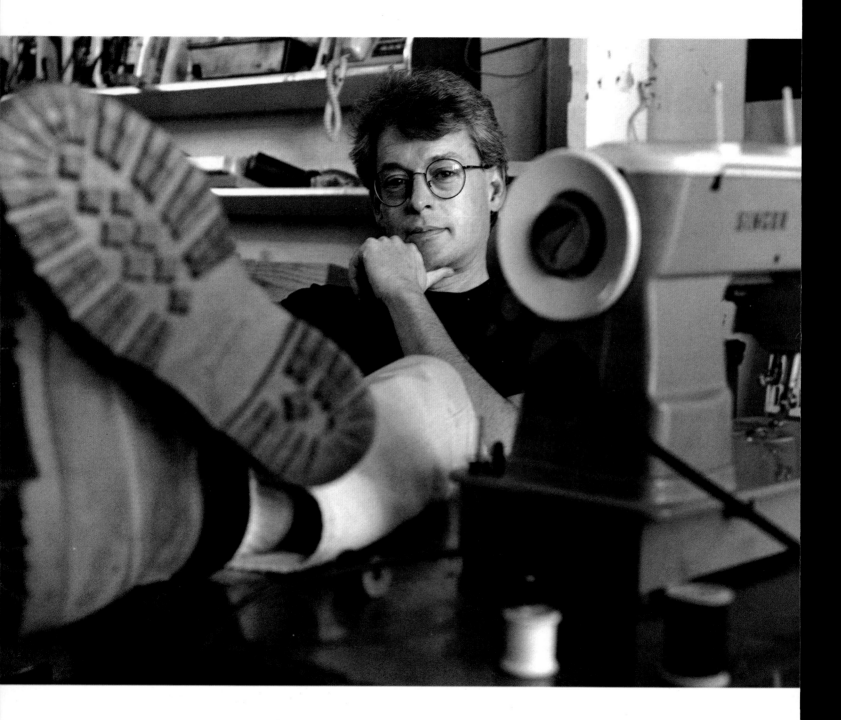

*Cleve Jones is the creator of the Names Project AIDS Memorial Quilt.*
*He always knew he was gay. As an adolescent he "hoped it would go away," and feared he would be*
*ostracized for the rest of his life. In high school, during a visit to the school library, Cleve found a mag-*
*azine story on gays, and it became his goal in life to go to a Gay Pride parade. At seventeen he hitch-*
*hiked to San Francisco, and he has been a gay activist ever since.*
*Cleve, thirty-eight, lives in Sonoma County, California. He was photographed at the Names Project*
*office in San Francisco.*

When I started the Quilt, I was looking for evidence. I remember standing at the corner of Castro and Market in 1985, and the headlines in the newspaper said that one thousand San Franciscans had already been killed by AIDS. And I thought if we could tear down these Victorian houses and the shops, if this were a meadow with one thousand corpses lying in the sun, then people would look at it, they would understand. And if they were human beings, they would be compelled to respond. But there was no such evidence. So I wanted to create a physical testimony. The three-by-six-foot panel is the approximate size of a grave, so when the Quilt is all laid out, one gets a sense of how many people have died.

In 1985, when we were getting ready for the annual candlelight tribute to Harvey Milk and George Moscone, my friend Joseph Durant and I got big pieces of cardboard and poster board and asked everybody to write down the name of one person they knew who had been killed by AIDS. Hundreds and then thousands of people made these signs. We walked down Market Street to city hall and then we continued on to the federal building. I had hidden extension ladders in the shrubbery around the building, and when we got there we put the ladders up against the wall and climbed three stories up with big rolls of tape. We covered the whole front facade of this gray stone building with the names of our dead.

It was a startling image, and people stood there in the cold for hours. Many people learned for the first time that they had already lost someone—an old roommate, or somebody they used to go dancing with. As I was looking at this sort of patchwork of names I said to myself, "It looks like a quilt." When I said the word *quilt*, I was immediately flooded with memories of my grandmother and my great-grandmother, who had sewn a series of quilts that have been passed down through the generations in my family. It was such a warm, middle-class, middle-America, nonthreatening, traditional-values sort of image. I thought, "Aha, this is the symbol to match with this disease that's killing faggots and junkies and black women and children and other people our society has not yet come to value." And that was the idea.

Then I talked about it with my friends and a whole year passed, and during that year I tested positive. I was attacked. And my very best friend, Marvin Feldman, was dying in Providence, Rhode Island. It was a really horrible winter, much like this past winter, with a lot of death. Then in the spring of '87, I made the first quilt, for Marvin. And it grew.

# JOHN BLANSETT AND HIS MOTHER, ANN

*John Blansett has lived all thirty-one years of his life in Mississippi, and believes he contracted HIV in his hometown of Okolona seven years ago. A former nurse's aide and insurance salesman, John rises at seven each morning, crochets afghans, and is "learning to cook all those things that my mother cooked when I was little—turnips, turnip greens, and pork chops."*

*John sits with his fifty-nine-year-old mother, Ann Blansett, during her lunch break from the furniture factory, located four blocks from the family's wooden frame house in the heart of town. The two were photographed in the dining room, where they eat together every day. Ann had just finished a white-bread, mayonnaise, and pineapple sandwich.*

*John:* Sometimes I get lonesome for a gay friend to talk to, but I still don't regret moving back home. What's really been ironic for me is the support I got and where it came from. I did not get support from any of my gay relatives or gay friends, but people I was sure would not even come in the room with me and share the same air turned out to be totally supportive.

I'd say nine out of ten people are well-enough educated, even here in Mississippi, to not be afraid of me. But that one person in ten can sure wreck your mental balance. It preys on you when you hear that an uncle or aunt is afraid to open a letter you've mailed to them. I've been asked to leave people's houses. That came as a big shock to me. It actually depressed me for a time.

Anyone who knows me knows that I'm HIV-positive. I didn't have to tell them a thing. I mean, one or two people found out, and that was all it took. The grapevine is quite effective.

There is a part of me that is still very, very grateful that I'm gay—very grateful because I was looking for anything to distinguish me from the prejudice and the bigotry and the good-old-boy mentality that infiltrates the South.

*Ann:* He told most everybody he was gay even before he got HIV-positive. I stand on firm ground. So people just don't bother me. But now there's a lot of people in the town that's gone out of their way to let me know that they like me and they like John. They didn't just come out and say it directly, but I knew and they knew.

But most of them are just dumb people that don't know any better. People are saying things, and not wanting their families coming around us. I've even got members of the family that don't come around anymore. But they don't say anything. They worry about their social standing and their church. Because they're associated with us, they are tarnished, I guess you might say.

I have one sister, she'll come over, but she never sits down. I don't lose any sleep over it.

*World War II Navy veteran Paul Hardman, seventy, is a founding member of the eight-year-old American Legion Post 448, the nation's only predominantly gay post.*
*Paul and his partner of forty years, Warren Kopp, sixty-three, live in the Pacific Heights section of San Francisco. Paul is a retired banker. He was photographed in the salon of their Victorian home next to a seventeenth-century bust of Louis XIV.*

Ten years ago it became apparent to me that the cutting edge for gay rights in the military had to be from the outside by those of us who had served honorably and successfully in the military—people who knew what it was like to be in the military but who were beyond their reach. We were now civilians, and I don't care how big a general you are, you are second-rate to a civilian. So I founded American Legion Post 448.

An American Legion post is a minimum of fifteen people who are honorably discharged war veterans who are interested in working with war veterans. It took a year and a half to get them to accept our application. Because we were gay, because we were making an outreach to gay and lesbian veterans, they didn't want our kind. Several times they lost our application.

They threw up every roadblock, creating things that were not really required. All of our members had to show formal discharge papers to at least two other members of the American Legion to make sure that we were truly veterans. We had to pick the name of an American war hero, which is also not required. So I picked Alexander Hamilton, because he was gay.

Many American Legion posts sit around and drink beer. They tell limited-intelligence jokes, talk dirty about girls, and make snide remarks about gay people and pretend to perform a lot of functions which are in their handbooks but don't actually occur. They have all kinds of subcommittees on youth, radio communication, and espionage. It's like a Boy Scout handbook that has very little relevance in actual practice. The intentions of those who put it together were good—but the phenomenon that's observable in actual conduct is not.

Before they really knew or had any experience with gay veterans, they were suspicious and antagonistic. People would ask, "Will your members dress funny and speak funny?"

We march in parades and we win their prizes—which is not really any comment on how good we are, but, frankly, how poor they are. When the veterans are all out marching, like on Memorial Day, we're there.

# GREG GREELEY

*In June 1991, on the day before he was scheduled to be discharged from active duty at the Pentagon, Air Force Captain Greg Greeley carried the banner that led the Gay Pride parade in Washington, D.C. His action caused a sensation, and the military held up his discharge by one day. He now serves as a reserve officer.*

*The twenty-seven-year-old is a computer specialist with a government contractor. He was photographed at his home in Arlington, Virginia.*

I liked the military. I was there because I felt that what we were doing was important—to protect the people here in the United States. This sounds corny, but I liked the fact that you were serving your country.

But I couldn't continue to do that and still remain in the closet. That was finally asking too much. I was so happy I was getting out. On Pride Day, I carried the banner in front of the parade. It was the first time that I had openly been associated with anything gay. It was our day. You could be out there in the sunshine rather than some dim bar.

Afterward, a friend asked if I was interested in talking with *The Washington Post,* and I said, "Sure." The next day there I was on the front page of the Metro section. The article started out with the words "Air Force Captain Greg Greeley . . . "

I nearly dropped the newspaper. I couldn't believe it. I had this vague hope that maybe no one at the Pentagon read the newspaper that day. When I was walking toward my office I had to go past my colonel's office, and he had five people in there Xeroxing the *Post.*

I went right into his office and I said, "I assume you've read the paper."

And he said, "Well, yes, and we guess it's about time you were leaving the service then, huh?" They were more than willing to continue the discharge like it was scheduled. Unfortunately, there were people in the Air Force who weren't. They wanted to punish me for trying to tweak their nose.

By 9:30 that morning they had put my discharge on hold. I had a very numb feeling. This was the thing that I'd worried about for four years. The thing that I always dreaded would happen happened. I had to report for an interview. It was like a cat-and-mouse game. What it boiled down to was, they wanted to know, was I gay. They said that since I wasn't answering their questions, they would have to open a full-blown investigation, and that could take weeks or months. And as long as they had me under investigation, I would be forced to stay in the service, and the worst part: they said if they found any evidence of

criminal behavior in my background, and they included sodomy, they would bring charges against me.

I knew that the deck was stacked against me—the only card I had in my favor was publicity. So I called anyone and everyone that I knew. The next day, I was trapped at work, and I really couldn't call anyone, but I couldn't help it if they called me. I was doing live radio interviews from my desk in the Pentagon. Then sometime between 11 A.M. and noon that day Defense Secretary Dick Cheney told the Air Force to let me go. By 2 P.M. that day, I had my discharge.

People go through a struggle in coming out. To have it done for you in one day was great.

FRANK KAMENY

*In 1957, Frank Kameny was dismissed from his civilian government job because he was gay. The World War II veteran with a Harvard Ph.D. fought his dismissal, but was unable to keep the job or get another in the burgeoning field of astronomy.*

*After his dismissal, Frank became obsessed with fighting for gay rights and against discriminatory federal employment practices. In 1961, he and about a dozen others formed the Mattachine Society of Washington, an affiliate of an early gay organization that had been started eleven years earlier in Los Angeles. At a time when others hid from government surveillance, Mattachine of Washington put FBI director J. Edgar Hoover on its mailing list, and the unsolicited copies of Mattachine's newsletter,* The Gazette, *caught the FBI off guard. Hoover demanded that his subscription be canceled. Mattachine members replied that they would remove Hoover's name from their list if he removed their names from the FBI's lists. Hoover's subscription continued until his death in 1972.*

*Frank was an early leader in disputing the belief, widely held even among fellow gays, that homosexuality was a sickness. Since 1968, he has worked full-time handling the cases of gays who have been denied security clearances or are facing clearance investigations or military discharge. At sixty-seven, Frank lives alone in Washington, D.C. He was photographed one afternoon while he worked in his home office.*

In the 1950s and '60s it was a much more repressive context. There were no protections. Whether it was federal employment or private employment, the general rule of thumb was that if you were known to be gay you didn't obtain or retain the job, period. In 1957, I was fired from the federal government on the grounds of being gay. That was all that was necessary. Being gay was the basis for total disqualification for federal civil service. There was nothing more that was needed.

I was an astronomer in the Army Map Service. At the time I lost my job, the space age was just barely opening up. Had I not been fired when I was, I would have shifted over to the newly formed NASA. I still like to have dreams that I might very well have been one of the astronauts. I would have loved that. That's one of the things that I regret. That all went down the drain.

I had never been one to slink around in a closet. They learned that I was gay, and proceeded to dismiss me. It's simply sheer, pure, unqualified, distilled, concentrated bigotry. I was the first who fought my dismissal all the way, including writing my own petition for the Supreme Court. The Supreme Court chose not to take the case.

I've always had a burning sense of justice. But, of course, there are too many injustices in the world. You can't address them all. I would not have felt right if I hadn't followed my own case to the end of the avenue. And even if my own personal case was over, well, we had to fight this. So I continued and got drawn into it. My feeling was that by taking cases I could cause changes. And in fact I did. The Civil Service Commission, which covered employment of all federal employees, said, "We will not hire gays." They don't have that policy anymore. I got rid of it after an eighteen-year fight. They made their announcement on July 3, 1975—announcing, in effect, not in these words, that they were changing their policy to suit me. They called me up in advance to tell me.

# JOSEPH DITTFELD

*Joseph Dittfeld was born Joseph Gabler, a Jew, in 1930 in Germany. When he was eight years old he was picked up by the Nazis and placed in a concentration camp. Through bribery, his family bought false Italian citizenship papers that gave Joseph his freedom and a new name: Dittfeld.*

*By the time he realized he was gay, Joseph had married, fathered a daughter, and divorced. He was photographed in his living room in New Orleans.*

Because of my experiences, I have never been afraid. The worst already happened to me. In late 1938, after *Kristallnacht*, I stayed with the nanny in Chemnitz, Germany. The early part of '39, several months after I stayed with her, the Nazis found out who I was and picked me up and took me to a camp.

I was eight. I knew what was happening. Eight-year-olds are not stupid. They picked me up with a lot of other people, put us on a truck, and took us to a train and took us to Leipzig, a collection camp. They numbered you, and collected you. They decided whether you should go to Auschwitz and be exterminated, or whether you should go to a labor camp as a slave.

I just don't think about it. But it never leaves your mind. That picture is there. The first experience I had in the camp, a woman went into labor. She was just lying on the ground and two Nazis came over, and as the baby was coming out they grabbed it and pulled it out and took the baby and slammed it against the wall. Killed it. And the woman bled to death.

I don't forget it. I mean you can't, but I don't think about it in my everyday life. After the whole thing was over, when I got off the boat in New York, the time was to make the decision to blot everything out and forget.

Until recently, the last time I was in synagogue was when they burned it in Chemnitz, on *Kristallnacht.* The rabbi died in it. My grandfather, my aunt, my uncle—we stood there on the street across from the synagogue. The Germans were there cheering the Nazis on.

I don't know what made me go back to the synagogue. It was probably a longing for tradition.

Tradition means a Jewish way of life. There's a Jewish way of doing things: a Jewish way of cooking, a Jewish way of praying, a Jewish way of gathering. Tradition. You don't do it necessarily because you believe in God. I don't believe in God at all. Sometimes I envy people that have that belief. I go to synagogue because I am a Jew. I was born a Jew. I belong to these people. It's something I have to pass on to my children, my children's children.

Just as the Jews are my people, the gays are my brothers and sisters. We, the Jews, wore the yellow star—the yellow star, which I wore, which my mother burned. They made the

gays wear a pink triangle, which I didn't see. Now, gays have adopted this pink triangle. I disagree with that, to be used as it is, to walk around with the pink triangle on the lapel. A lot of people see the connection with the current persecution of gays and the extermination that the Nazis did. But it really doesn't fall into the same category. You take a group of people and you stick them in an oven—against being discriminated in housing. You can't just put the two together in the same category. You just can't do it.

We have to put it in perspective. It is discrimination, period. And in this day and age, in this country, in this state, there shouldn't be any. Discrimination in any form is just not acceptable. "We are all created equal." That's the way it should be. Sadly enough, we are not.

RAY HAGEN

*The early morning of June 28, 1969, Ray Hagen was in the Stonewall Inn when it was raided by New York City police. Ray had been caught by raids before, once bribing a policeman with his watch in order to avoid arrest. But this raid was different, because gays fought back. Gay Pride parades across the nation commemorate the event each year.*

*Ray has worked as an actor and dabbled in play writing. Now fifty-five, he records books for the blind at the Library of Congress. He was photographed in his Washington, D.C., apartment.*

For all of the liberations that were going on in the 1960s, gays were not part of it. It was still the thing that "dared not speak its name." You had your life with your job and your friends, and then you had your sex life. Secret. Very secret. Very much apart. You got your sex where you could find it—theater balconies, restrooms, certain street corners late at night.

You didn't find it, openly at least, at work. No flirting. You couldn't even talk about your dates to your co-workers without changing pronouns all the time. You couldn't find it in any of the "normal" places, so you found it where you could, and you were always apt to be caught by a plainclothesman. Always sneaking, hoping nobody you knew would see you.

My whole memory of bars is that they all were very dark, and that was part of it, because we knew when we walked in what might happen. The owners of the gay bars had an arrangement: they paid off the cops to stay off their tails. And if they missed a payment, in came the cops. They weren't interested in jailing criminals—just taking the money: "Pay me not to arrest you, you faggot."

When the cops came, suddenly the lights would go on. Everybody'd start to act "normal." And made sure their chairs were moved far enough away so that it wouldn't look as though they were a couple. Or everybody suddenly just looking nowhere, not relating to anybody else and keeping an eye on what the cops were doing. Because we'd all been through this before; we knew the choreography.

I'd only been to the Stonewall maybe twice before. I went because they had dancing there, and that was very unusual for gay bars. There was a commotion that had started in the bar section, so everybody went to look. People were screaming in these cops' faces and pushing them on the shoulder. You never did that with the police. A homosexual doing that to a cop? Are you insane?

There was a lot of yelling; mostly it was just variations on the "pig" theme. There was a lot of pushing. I was suddenly in the middle of it. There was a lot of adrenaline, because we were fighting, and I think it was the first time the cops found out what it's really like when you get a bunch of queens really ticked off. Anything that wasn't nailed to the floor was being hurled. The adrenaline, the energy, the rage that had been kept in all this lifetime. The cops were being beaten up by all these pansies. We were fighting. Gay men had fought for the women's movement. White people had fought for the black movement. It never occurred to us that we had a movement too. That's how ingrained it was. It never occurred to us. It wasn't even something we dreamed about.

# ROBERTA ACHTENBERG

*Assistant Secretary of Housing and Urban Development Roberta Achtenberg is the first openly gay person to be confirmed by the U.S. Senate for a high-level government position. As do most nominees, at her Senate hearing Roberta introduced her partner: Mary Morgan, a San Francisco Municipal Court judge, whom she has been with for eleven years. Senator Jesse Helms (Republican of North Carolina) sat in on the hearing and later vowed to hold up the nomination; he was quoted as calling Roberta a "damn lesbian." The heated Senate floor debate, in which Roberta and her family were personally attacked, stretched over three days. Roberta was confirmed in May 1993 by a vote of fifty-eight to thirty-one.*

*Roberta, forty-two, and Mary, forty-seven, are both attorneys. They and their seven-year-old son, Benjamin Achtenberg, moved to Washington from San Francisco, where Roberta had been a member of the board of supervisors since 1990. Mary now teaches law at the American University.*

*Roberta was photographed as she was sworn in before the Senate Banking Committee confirmation hearing in April. Mary is to the left.*

*In her statement before the committee, Roberta said, "My parents came to this country believing if they worked hard enough, they would succeed. They sent their children to college, even though they never even went to high school. My parents endured discrimination so that their children might be free. The privileges I enjoy by virtue of their hard work impose upon me an obligation—not just to take care of myself, and not just to provide for my loved ones and my child; but to contribute my skills and my energy to the well-being of the community."*

Everybody has an obligation to perform public service. By *public service* I do not mean hold a public office or something like that. What it needs to have is some sense that people are making some kind of contribution that makes the world a little better off than it would have been. It's not just good enough to give and take with no net effect. This is just my way of making my contribution.

At the hearing, I didn't even know that Jesse Helms was there. Anytime you go into a courtroom you focus on the people who you want to persuade, who you want to make eye contact with, with whom you want to establish a connection. So he was not of concern to me.

MS. ACHTENBERG

What was important to me about that day—having been nominated by the president to hold a high government position, having had the trust of the president to nominate me, being able to demonstrate my qualifications for the job to the Banking Committee, being sworn in to give testimony in my own behalf to hold the most important public position I have had the opportunity as of this date to hold—that's what I was there for. That's what was important to me about that day.

I would introduce my family as I did. I've been out so long, I don't really consider it an issue anymore. I live my life the way I live my life. I accept other people for what they are. Whether they can act similarly is basically their problem.

# RAFAEL AND ANA CHANG

*Rafael Chang, thirty-one, and Ana Chang, thirty-two, are brother and sister. Their parents fled Communist China in the early 1950s, moving first to Honduras and then to the United States.*
*Ana is a courier. Rafael works for the Asian Pacific AIDS Coalition. They were photographed in the garden at Rafael's home in San Francisco.*

*Rafael:* We were supposed to have lunch with my parents. We were in the kitchen. My mom was cooking. My sister started it. She began trying to explain that we were gay. Given the number of languages that we spoke at home—from Chinese to Spanish to broken English—the communication was a little hard. We finally ended up having to use the Chinese-English dictionary to explain.

*Ana:* We didn't know the Chinese word for being gay. So we had to look up *homosexual.* And we had to point at it. Dad was the one who read it off and interpreted it for my mom.

*Rafael:* At that point my mom stopped cooking, and finally got what we were saying. She started to cry and started screaming. My dad sort of shut down emotionally, and was very confused. He started questioning: "Are you sure?"—the whole business. And my mom asked whether we wanted to see a psychiatrist.

We ended up screaming and trying to explain. I sort of got fed up, and I left and sat in the car. I had expected some grief around it, but not this much. That was the one point I wished I wasn't gay.

*Ana:* I was trying to explain our side so that I could feel at peace. But my mother is a very stubborn woman. So after a while, we both acknowledged that we weren't getting anywhere. I left.

*Rafael:* After that we exchanged letters. We tried calling, but my mom would get hysterical and hang up the phone. They were very angry, disappointed, and, on some level, shameful. In the Chinese culture, not only are you shaming your parents, you're shaming your grandparents, your great-grandparents, and your great-great-grandparents. If you do something bad it reflects on your family and on your grandparents, even though they're dead.

The final letter was: as soon as I'm willing to change my mind around being gay, then I'm welcome back into the family. And that sort of tore it for me. For about two to three years, I disowned being Chinese, because being Chinese meant that I would have a family, or a set of parents to take care of me. Those years were the hardest, because for us it was mandatory to attend family holidays, religious holidays, whatever. Whenever the Chinese New Year came around, or someone's birthday came around, we weren't with our families. We tried really hard to make sure that we took care of each other, and we still do. Family is still very important to me.

*Ana:* When I'm around other Asians I find myself a bit distanced. They haven't lost what I have lost. They don't know what it's like to live my life without a family. I wouldn't trade places with them. I feel very happy with who I am. If I could choose whether I could be straight or gay, I wouldn't change. I would rather be gay. I couldn't have grown as a person in the same way if I was straight.

Like my brother, I have had to form my own family, and these people that I consider my family will be there, and we're not even connected by blood.

*Rafael:* It's really come full circle. For me, it's about some very strong self-acceptance. I really wouldn't change anything.

# FAYBELL MA-HEÉ

*Faybell Ma-Heé, twenty, founded a women's theater company in 1991 in Atlanta called Silver Fingers. The twenty women in the fledgling company strive to present new works by and about African American women.*
*She was photographed in her home in Atlanta.*

Up until recently I was a telemarketer. That had gotten on my nerves, and I now make a living as an artist. If it was not for the support of my former lover, I would not be able to do that. I would be waiting tables somewhere.

A theater company can solely be defined by its mission. It's important to make sure that women have a voice and platform. We don't allow men to participate in the crew. As a feminist I put money into the women's community before I put it outside of it, especially when it comes to hiring technical people. Women that are technical people get passed up for tech work because it's the "male" end of theater. And I have to make sure women get supported first. We have decided that men can participate as actors. We do this to get the full range of women's experiences viewing the productions. Our main goal is to be a mirror image of life as it relates to women.

My main focus as a lesbian and as a feminist is to build alliances across sexuality. Interestingly enough, we've been able to maintain a sexual-preference parity in all of our productions: at least half the cast is lesbian and half the cast is heterosexual. The real work is often not onstage. The real process is for the women who choose to participate, and the process of doing the production. I can't tell you how many times our rehearsals have been rap sessions. Everyone comes, and we all learn about each other.

*Phyllis Lyon, sixty-eight, and Del Martin, seventy-one, are best known as two of the eight women who founded the Daughters of Bilitis in 1955. At the time there were two other gay groups in the United States: the Mattachine Society and ONE, Inc. Daughters of Bilitis was the first exclusively lesbian organization. Chapters spread across the nation, and the group flourished in the 1960s, holding national conventions and garnering the attention of the mainstream media and the FBI. The national organization dissolved in 1970. Today, only the Boston chapter remains.*

*The two continue to work for women's and gay rights. They coauthored* Lesbian/Woman *in 1972, and Del wrote* Battered Wives *in 1976.*

*The couple of more than forty years first met when they worked for construction-industry trade publications in Seattle, Washington. Del was the first person Phyllis had ever met who she knew was a lesbian. They later moved to San Francisco, and they still live in the house they bought there in 1955. Del is divorced, with one daughter and two grandchildren. The two were photographed with their cat, Koala, in their kitchen.*

*Phyllis:* We had a phone call from one lesbian. She wanted to know if we would be interested in helping to start a social group for lesbians. So we said yes.

*Del:* Everybody was very isolated and closeted. It was difficult to find people to join. We came up with the name Daughters of Bilitis so we would sound like a women's lodge—Daughters of the Nile or Daughters of the American Revolution—and nobody would know that it was a lesbian group.

*Phyllis:* Some had wanted to make it like a women's lodge where you would have ritual membership induction and things along those lines. The rest of us didn't really go for that idea exactly. Another woman brought the *Songs of Bilitis* to our attention. It was a lesbian narrative poem. She felt that lesbians would know what Daughters of Bilitis meant, but nobody else would. Of course, I don't think most of the lesbians knew what it meant either. We had never heard of this poem.

We decided we needed a newsletter. With the very first issue we had about 175 copies before the Mattachine Society's mimeograph broke down. A lot of members of DOB didn't use their real names. I became Ann Ferguson. I was editor of *The Ladder,* our newsletter. I guess it was the idea that my name was going to be in print, and I thought, "Somebody might see it and God knows what would happen, so I'd better not do that." So I took my middle name and my mother's maiden name.

Then at the same time we started the newsletter in 1956, we started our public discussion meetings. We rented a room downtown, and people could just come by. People would want to meet Ann Ferguson because they'd seen *The Ladder* so they'd want to meet the editor. So Del would yell, "Ann Ferguson! Ann! Ann!" And I would never respond, because it wasn't my name.

Then she'd say, "Phyllis!" and I would turn right around. So we decided that the pseudonym thing was really ridiculous, and we killed Ann Ferguson.

# THE HENSONS

*Brenda and Wanda Henson of Gulfport, Mississippi, have been together for nine years. They live two blocks from the Gulf of Mexico and next door to Brenda's mother.*

*Wanda, thirty-eight, is a native of the state, having grown up forty miles away in Pascagoula. Brenda, forty-seven, was born in Ohio and moved to Mississippi in 1981. Both are divorced, and each has two grown children. Both are studying for their doctorates in adult education at the University of Southern Mississippi. They hope their formal education will help them with Sister Spirit, a nonprofit organization they created to address more than twenty social issues including sexism, racism, homophobia, ageism, peace, and housing.*

*Brenda and Wanda also produce the Gulf Coast Women's Festival, run a food bank, and operate a secondhand store called Leftovers. Brenda and Wanda were photographed in the store.*

*Brenda:* When I finally got divorced, I wanted my name changed. I changed it to Henson. Henson is my mother's birth name. I was going to graduate from junior college, and I wanted my diploma to say "Henson" instead of my birth name, or the married name that I'd had. Then some time later, Wanda decided that she wanted the name too.

*Wanda:* I was raised with very traditional family values, and I just thought that, well, Brenda had changed her name. She had been married four times and didn't want to have any of the names that had been tacked onto the back of her name. I had been married at one point in my life too, and I didn't want to take my maiden name back. So I went and I talked to Brenda's mother, and I said, "I'm just very traditional in thinking, and I would like for me and Brenda, our family, to have a family name. Since Henson is the name she has chosen, then I would like to be a Henson."

And her mother started crying, and she said, "Oh, this is wonderful."

*Brenda:* Everyone assumes that we're sisters.

*Wanda:* We look nothing alike.

*Brenda:* It's a perception, it's automatic: two old-maid sisters living down here.

*Wanda:* We had to go to school to get our transcripts. We're standing at the window, and Brenda applied to get her transcript before I did. So Brenda gets her transcript; then I step up and the woman looks at me and she says: "Well, is she your mother?" Brenda's nine years older than I am.

I said, "No, she's not."

"Oh, well, is she your sister?" the woman asked.

I said, "No ma'am, she's not."

And she said, "Well, what relationship is she to you?"

She was getting a little bit edgy with me. And I said, "She's my lover."

And the woman got stiff as could be and said, "Well! Wait a minute. That's cool!" She said the word *cool* like we did in the seventies. I think she was scared.

So then we go back again to register for school in the fall. And she remembers our names out of all of those students: "Hensons, right?"

*Neighbors in New Orleans call Dewain Belgard the Saint Francis of Chartres Street, for his is the home to dozens of abandoned animals. His menagerie includes a dog that can't walk and pigeons that can't fly. He is a vegetarian and a Buddhist.*

*Dewain is the regional administrator for a substance abuse clinic. He is forty-eight and was photographed getting a kiss from his inherited dog, Girly.*

At a very, very early age, I can remember hunting at night. I'm not quite sure it was legal—spotlighting. We were flashing the light all the time in the trees, and when you catch the eyes, it's like two bright spots suddenly appear. You can't see the animal; you just see the eyes. They're brilliant. Cat eyes and dog eyes are the same thing in darkness: if light hits them from a particular direction, they appear to be neon. So that's what you see—those green dots there. You shoot at that.

My father spotted an opossum up in a persimmon tree out in a swamp, and handed me the rifle. I must have been six, and I shot it and—because I was a good shot—killed it. It fell. It just fell right out of the tree onto the ground. Dead. I remember the terrible feeling of stroking it. Still very warm, of course. And very, very fuzzy. I had a very, very bad feeling. Which I didn't understand until years later.

We just left it there. We didn't eat them. There was no sense to it at all. Just to see if you were a good enough shot to kill it. In the country a rite of passage was to kill things.

I have ten cats right now. I've got six dogs and two lovebirds, four pigeons: so, a total of twenty-two.

Blanche, the black cat, comes from a friend who died of AIDS. He and his partner had seven cats. They all were taken to the pound. It's possible that some of them got homes. But most of them got killed within five days. Blanche was the only one I could take in, and I took her because I had promised him specifically that I would not let Blanche go. He'd had her for many, many years. She was his first cat.

Alice the cat is also from someone who died. These were animals that I knew, so in some cases I specifically went and got them to avoid them going to the pound. In many ways the animals become children surrogates. I think that's particularly true of gay people, and also heterosexual couples who've chosen not to have children, or who can't have children. Sometimes their pets are their children.

But there comes a time when you can't really take in any more. I just have to pass them up. It's a real conflict with people. I think most people don't feel the tension, because they're simply callous themselves: they close their eyes to suffering, even of other people, much less other animals.

To me the in-between road is to be able to see the suffering and feel it, and then do something when you can, and when you can't, you just hurt.

# RAINEY CHEEKS

*Albert "Rainey" Cheeks, forty, has lived in Washington, D.C., all his life. An ordained minister who has worked as a pipe fitter, karate instructor, and bar manager, Rainey has been HIV-positive for eight years. His lover of six years died of AIDS in 1984.*
*He was photographed in his home.*

I am in a holistic therapy group for people with HIV. It's my health maintenance program. Part of the problem of health is people simply take one approach. I take a real comprehensive approach: acupuncture is part, sitting in the sunlight is part, drinking herbal tea is another part. I don't leave it to one system. The only system I try to stay away from is allopathic medicine—drugs.

My belief is that if you clean the body out, give the body the nutrients it needs, then the body will heal itself. So far, I've been right.

My grandmother and my mother worked with herbs. I use combinations of herbs, and I try to drink thirty-two ounces of tea a day. I use pokeweed, which grows wild on the side of the road. It grows tall, and has little berries on it. They're dark purple berries. But you have to be careful about pokeberry. It's poisonous, so you have to know how to cook it. I make a tea out of it. You boil the leaves, pour the water off of it first, then you go back and boil it again. It will fight off viruses and everything.

It's a very simple system that says, "Clean out your body." So don't eat junk food; don't put anything in your body that your body is going to have to struggle with.

No AZT, no DDI. I won't say never, but as it stands right now, I cannot imagine a reason why I would go on these drugs. I look at what it does to the body, and I am just not willing to go through that.

Somewhere along the line you have to look up and laugh about it, and you move on. Look at HIV. It's not my enemy, it's just a reminder. It's there to say, "Okay, you survived for eight years, but how did you survive? You choose these foods, you drink these herbs, you do this acupuncture, you will not hang around certain people. Now go ahead and break those rules and I will take over."

We have to look at the difference between healing and curing. People want to be cured because people want to say, "Fix me so I can get up and go do what I used to do." Healing says, "No. Learn why you got in this position. Life has so much to offer. God gives us all life, but it's up to you to live." I take the challenge to live.

DELTA LAMBDA PHI

*The Omega chapter of the predominantly gay fraternity Delta Lambda Phi was founded in Tucson at the University of Arizona's thirty-five-thousand-student campus in 1991. President Chris Olson, twenty, was among the first students to join the new fraternity as a member of the Alpha pledge class. Five of the ten members of the fraternity were photographed in Chris's dorm room. They are, from left to right: Oscar Ulloa, Jonathan Zenz, Chris Olson, Chris Mayor, and Joe Galvan.*

*Chris Olson:* I almost rushed Sigma Chi. That's the most prestigious frat on campus. My grandfather was a Chi Phi, so I had a legacy there. I could have easily, with my grades, gotten into another fraternity if I had wanted to. But I didn't. I had thought that a lot of the Greeks here are really very superficial, very elitist. But since I went through the pledge program at Delta Lambda, I have a lot more respect for the Greek people on campus. I always thought it was just a friendly little thing where you basically pay to have more friends. But it's not; it really does create really strong bonds. There's a lot of work involved; their pledge programs are incredibly tough.

Some gays and lesbians say that our fraternity can be somewhat elitist. We try not to be, but it's part of being a fraternity. You give bids out to people you would want to be part of a group. Most people are used to clubs where you just show up and you're part of it. This is a lot more; it's a big commitment.

It's okay that we date inside the fraternity, and it's not a casual thing if we date. It's pretty serious, actually. But we do not sleep with pledges. It can be considered hazing. We have a standards committee that deals with stuff like that. The guy who did it once had to do a service project.

The makeup of the fraternity is just like any other fraternity. We all have big brothers. We have our ceremonies, but we're not supposed to talk about that. I wear my sweatshirt a lot. We try to wear them as much as we can, but we don't have as many members as all the other fraternities, so we aren't as visible. But whenever I wear it, I get response. Basically most people know what Delta Lambda Phi is—especially for people who know the Greek alphabet. The fraternities don't like to share that bond with us, because they're kind of phobic.

Sororities have been really good. Our pledge class was having their retreat, and about ten Alpha Phis came over and we went out for yogurt. It was really fun. Just talk, talk, talk the whole time. They said, "You guys are more like sorority girls than fraternity guys." I think that was kind of funny.

Our Alpha class song was based on "Express Yourself," by Madonna. It was like, "Don't go for those other fraternity boys, go for us, we'll take you on platonic dates. We'll bring you home early, we won't try to feel up your skirt . . . " We got to serenading a bunch of sororities with it. They loved it. Except their boyfriends, when their boyfriends were there, and they heard it, were like, "Oh." They were kind of scared of us. Because it also had a section that said, "We see all these Fiji boys at our bars. . . . Don't go for a Kappa Sig, baby, put your love to the test, you know, you know, you've got to . . . dump all those fraternity boys and go for Delta Lambda Phi."

# BRUCE HAYES

*Bruce Hayes started swimming at age six when he and his older sister joined their neighborhood swim team. By the time he was in high school, Bruce was diving into a chilly pool each morning at 5:15 and swimming almost six hours each day.*

*In the 1984 Olympics, Bruce swam the anchor leg of the eight-hundred-meter freestyle relay, capturing the gold medal with a world-record time and beating the opponent by four-hundredths of a second. The heated race made front page headlines the next day and was one of the highlights of the Los Angeles Olympics.*

*Bruce left competition in 1985 as he began to explore his sexual orientation. Then in 1990, Bruce swam in the Gay Games, which put him back in the news because he is one of only a handful of openly gay world-class athletes.*

*Bruce, thirty, works at a large public relations agency in Manhattan. He was photographed while doing laps at his twice-weekly practice with Team New York Aquatics.*

I began suspecting I was gay when I went to college, but I really repressed it. Swimming was a good way to do that because I had my head in the water six hours a day. I just didn't think about it. Swimming provided a convenient excuse. I certainly was aware that I was attracted to other men at that time. But that was too scary a thought to actually put into action. I was in an environment, sports, which is very homophobic, very competitive, and very cutthroat in many ways. It's not something I thought I could handle and compete at the same time.

I swam through the spring of 1985 at UCLA. I swam one more season and that was only to fulfill my scholarship requirement. I stopped at that point, and a large part of the reason I stopped was the fact that I was gay. I felt that if I was going to figure out what was going on in my personal life, I couldn't do that and swim at the same time. The other thing was I just felt that I had accomplished pretty much everything I wanted to in swimming and there wasn't any challenge left for me that would keep me in it.

I thought about swimming in the Olympics when I was a kid, of course. I would watch them incessantly. I remember watching the '72 Olympics when Mark Spitz swam. I would visualize what it would be like to be up on the medal stand and have the national anthem play. It was just a fantasy at that point; it wasn't something I really saw myself doing.

Then in 1984 when they played the national anthem, it's so many different things all at one time. It was very moving. At the same time, it's a relief that you feel, because there is

so much pressure that when it's finally over and you succeeded, you feel a weight lifted off your shoulders.

When I was standing up there I was thinking most, "God, I can't believe I did this." All those times I wondered whether it was worth it, getting up so early in the morning and going and swimming in a cold pool. There were so many times when I thought, "What am I doing? I could be having a social life, I could be going out with my friends." It just all felt worthwhile when you're standing up there on the medal stand.

GLENN BURKE

*Baseball folklore credits Glenn Burke and fellow Los Angeles Dodger Dusty Baker with creating the "high five" after the two hit back-to-back home runs in 1977.*

*Glenn, forty, played his first game at age eleven in a T-shirt league in Oakland, California. In 1972 he turned away college basketball and baseball scholarships to sign with the Dodgers. He played on their farm teams until first reaching the majors in 1976. He played for the Dodgers in the 1977 World Series. He was one of the club's top prospects, and, according to Glenn, they offered him a bonus if he would get married. The following year he was traded to his hometown Oakland A's. Two years later, after a knee injury and personal time off, Glenn's contract was not renewed.*

*Since he left professional baseball, Glenn has worked odd jobs. He was photographed at a gay softball league game in San Francisco, where he plays left field for a team sponsored by a sports bar called Uncle Bert's Place.*

In 1975, I knew that I was gay. I never knew before that, because I wasn't having sex with women or men. I was just playing sports. But I knew I was missing something in my life. I was missing a relationship, or a friendship with somebody special. All the other ballplayers had girlfriends or whatever. They were always hugging, and stuff, and I thought, "Why don't I feel like that?"

The first time it registered that I liked men I was in a mixed bar and there were men dancing with men. I said, "Ah-hah, I finally found it." I thought I was the only gay person in the world.

It was tough in baseball. They were setting me up with all these women. Women were around all the time. People asked me what was the matter: "I introduced you to the girl." I said, "I met her, but I had something else to do."

They never harassed me. But when they found out I was gay they were shocked. The ball players were like, "Glenn Burke gay? Him, walking through the locker room like King Kong?" They called me that because I was big. All I was doing was mocking them, walking through all butch. But when they found out, they froze in their shadows. I got along with everybody. I've always been able to play; I always felt I'd be one of the starting players on the team. No matter what team I'd get on, I'd be good enough to play.

I kept saying to myself, "As long as I bat three hundred, and do what I have to do, they can't say nothing." I had to be a little bit better just in case they did find out. I was always thinking about it.

In 1978, when I got traded to the Oakland A's, a player came up to me and said, "They're talking and saying that you're gay. I don't care if you are or not, you're still my friend." You can imagine how that made me feel. So I didn't find out until after I got to Oakland that the gossip was I was gay and that's why the Dodgers traded me.

It takes a lot to play professional baseball. It was more fun getting there than being there.

# AT THE CROSSROADS

*Charles "Butch" Graham, forty, the middle child of eleven siblings, says his parents were moonshiners and he has always been attracted to bars. He and his lover of three years, Jimmy Cason, thirty-two, run a pair of gay bars, Crossroads and Ollie Mae's, near Meridian, Mississippi.*
*Butch has run other bars. His last, called Poppers, was closed in 1987 after a petition of two hundred Meridian residents and a nightly stakeout at the bar ended in violence. The police declared the bar a public nuisance.*
*Jimmy and Butch were photographed outside of Ollie Mae's, a bar Butch named in honor of his mother.*

There were twenty-one days of siege. Whole families would come. It was twenty people, then thirty, and then forty. Every night. They'd call you "faggot." Every day I would get hit with one or two eggs. I'd get yellow on the back of my head. They'd run my business off so just four or five people would come to the bar. We didn't leave anytime sooner than one o'clock because I wasn't going to be closing down and going home because they were forcing us to.

They'd bust out windows, the Christians, setting up there preaching on the Bible. They called it a "fag bar," a "queer bar," an "AIDS factory." They'd use paint pellets—paint spots all over the wall in red, blues, yellows. They wrote "AIDS factory" on the side of the building. I wouldn't paint the building. It stayed up twenty-one days. The owner of the building offered me back my rent, my lease, and everything else to get me out of the building, because they were threatening to burn it down.

On the last night, the general mood was good. We'd been threatened with baseball bats and shotguns and everything else, and now we were talking one-on-one in the street. Then this guy, speaking in tongues, comes through the crowd with a baseball bat. My friend picked up the camcorder, cut it on, and was getting it up, and the guy hit the camera. Then someone hit somebody else behind the head with a baseball bat. I got hit. Then the police finally came. Down at the station everybody was charging everybody else.

The next day I got a hand-delivered letter from the chief of police to cease business for public welfare. So it was better to attack good old Butch than to tell all those citizens they were wrong. The city allowed people to destroy a business. It could have been Jewish, it could have been Baptist or Catholic or whatever. It was a business. It just depends on what you are fighting for. The bar was not a major factor. I just wasn't going to allow them to just run me off.

Even today, out here at Crossroads, I still lose mailboxes about every three weeks. I still lose signs. I've been shot at. When I first opened up out here, they shot my car up in the

parking lot and set my house on fire. Threw gasoline up on the side of it and threw a match on it.

I found out who they were, because they were running their mouths. And one thing about it: you just never know where gay people are, and if you keep quiet about it the information's going to come back to you. I ain't going to tell you what I did. Now they know that if you mess with me I will come and mess with you.

*Charles Hickman, thirty-one, grew up in rural Shuqualak, Mississippi. After college he moved to At-*
*lanta, but his heart remains in the country. Charles is a window installer. He spends his spare time*
*roaming the countryside in search of gay men and lesbians, listening to their stories, learning how*
*they live. He is also cochairman of the Atlanta chapter of Black and White Men Together.*
*Charles was photographed between two windows filled with the wintered kudzu vines that have*
*taken over this building and much of the South.*

The South tends to take its eccentrics in and not exclude them. One of the things that I
think has shielded gay folk in the country is that we have been viewed as eccentric. Small-
town life is almost like a village. You can't exclude an able-bodied participant in the community, so you make room, you make allowances, and they are a part of the community
fabric.

I guess maybe that is true with communities outside the South, but I think the South in
particular has been known for that, and that has been a protection for many gay people. I
know people who have been extremely flamboyant in their hometowns, but they haven't
been beaten or they are not verbally harassed every time they slip out their door. They
work. They go to church. They go to the grocery store. They do everything that everyone
else does. Everyone knows what is going on. People make do.

People are extremely adaptable, and it's comforting to me to listen to people and find
strategies of survival in the rural South. I never know when I might get tired of city living,
and it would be comforting to me to know that I can find a place to be myself but also be
a part of the community fabric.

# JOHN WILSON

*While director of the New Orleans City Planning Commission, John Wilson achieved notoriety when he was named Mr. Leather New Orleans. His picture appeared in local gay newspapers and later in the mainstream media. Many saw his conduct as unbecoming to his office, but John says he would have been applauded if his title had been won in a straight bodybuilding contest. A year later John resigned from his position, and from the department he had served for twenty-one years.*
*John, forty-six, lives in his native city with his lover of fourteen years, Mike Edwards, forty-two. John was photographed in his living room.*

My racial identity is something that's always been with me. I have experienced racial prejudice from time to time throughout my childhood and my adulthood.

As a child, friends would call me a "white peck," which is the term that they would use with light-skinned blacks. Uptown, where I lived most of my childhood, was black—dark skinned—and I was the minority. They'd say, "Oh, you know he's passing for white." The Creoles would call you *"passé blanc."*

I can't imagine what life would be like if people did not realize what I am, as far as being black as well as being gay. Some of the black gays were probably wondering why I would have an interracial relationship. I think the majority of them understood and appreciated it, but some of them did not. They may have wondered, because of my light complexion, if I'm just gravitating toward these Caucasians. I had, in fact, dated black men in previous years.

When you look at interracial couples themselves, they have a lot to deal with, and if you're gay and if you have an interracial relationship, I think there are some pressures that you're dealing with doublefold by being gay.

If there are two men together in public it doesn't really peg them as being gay. Or two black women living together, or two white women living together, is accepted because it's okay from an economic standpoint. Again, women have tended over the years to have a lower income and economic standard, and it's always kind of been accepted for two single women to share a household together. But then you have a black woman and a white woman living together; then I think a question mark comes into play. Again, that goes back to the racial prejudices, and you can't hide yourself quite as well. You can't explain it away: "Well this is my sister, this is my aunt," or whatever. It just is not as easy.

*Steve Takemura, twenty-nine, is the cochair of the five-hundred-member all-male Gay Asian and Pacific Alliance in San Francisco. He is director of administration for Canal Community Alliance, a multicultural social service agency in San Rafael, California, and is on the boards of five community nonprofit organizations.*

*Steve lives in Marin County, California, and was photographed at the entrance to GAPA's office.*

My mother and father were in an internment camp for four years—'41 to '45. They never talked about it. I had to read books, talk to other people, to learn about the camps. My seventh-grade teacher said that the Japanese were interned and it was justified for their own good, their own protection. I bought into that because my parents never talked about it. I look back at that moment and it just makes me want to fight more, to make America acknowledge what a mistake that was. It makes me want to fight for civil rights. It makes me angry.

I get my energy from watching *The 700 Club* every morning. I listen to the things they have to say at 7 A.M. It makes me so angry. At first I didn't want to watch it because it made me feel so helpless. Now I channel that energy into letter-writing and organizing.

It's really difficult for me being a person of color and gay. I don't really feel accepted in the Asian community because I am gay, and I don't really feel accepted in the lesbian and gay community either. They see me as Asian.

When I came out, I thought it would be some sort of utopia in the gay community. On my twenty-first birthday, a friend suggested a few bars to me, and they happened to be bars patroned by Asians and people who like Asians specifically. I wanted to go out to other bars. He flatly told me, "If you really want to meet somebody, I suggest you go to these specific bars."

I refused. I was going to go to any bar I wanted to go to just in protest. And you know what? I didn't meet anybody. He was right: I was ignored. I was shocked that there is that underlying segregation. Of course, there is no law. You can go to any bar that you want. But society and the greater community kind of dictates where you can go and where you can't go.

When I have dated people who have been non-Asian, their friends would actually go up to them and say, "I didn't know you were a rice queen," or "I didn't know you were into rice." They would say it jokingly, but it's really an insult. I would get ignorant things like "How come you don't know how to use chopsticks?" Or "How come you don't speak Japanese?" And it's like, "Well, I am fourth-generation. How come you don't speak German?" I am constantly finding people putting me in a stereotype. I am constantly asked, "Where are you from?"—like, where are you *really* from?

There are a lot of stereotypes of people, and unfortunately, these stereotypes have been carried on to the gay and lesbian community. We all need to look at racism within ourselves and address that. This is a great community, and we can't afford to alienate our own. It may take a lifetime, or two lifetimes, but we need to start the process and go forward.

# MARY COURTLAND

*Although Mary Courtland likes to tell people she is just shy of eighty, she is actually closer to ninety. She lives alone in a wooden farmhouse with an attached barn—a home filled with precious objects that visitors are instructed to note: family photos, certificates, hand-painted birds.*

*At the age of three, Mary and her family emigrated from Czechoslovakia to the United States. Mary lived more than half her life in the Midwest, working in blue-collar jobs—as a domestic, a "beauty operator," and a factory worker making Sears catalogs. She even spent time in a convent.*

*It has been only in the past twenty years that she has found a lesbian community. Her gay friends in Waldo County, Maine, watch out for her, taking her to the doctor, dentist, or grocery store.*

*She was photographed in her kitchen.*

I tried to be nice to men. I even went out with one or two, because that was what you were supposed to do. I went out two or three times, but when they tried to smooch with me, I'd be thinking of someone else, some woman I liked.

The word "gay" wasn't used then. I don't like it now. They use a lot of gay words when I read. Now they have "gay men" and "gay women." I think the best thing is "friend," "good friend," "very good friend"—you know what kind of friend.

My gosh, I've never lived with anybody, but I was hoping to. My first girlfriend was when I was about fourteen, fifteen years old. I had been put on the job taking care of kids. She lived in the house, upstairs with her mother. I've got pictures of her. She had long curls. I was too bashful. I never talked to her. I just walked around her. And that was my first girl, but she didn't know it. I didn't even know what was the matter with me.

Then I really fell for a girl who wasn't to be loved. She was working in the church. She was a sister—a sister in the church. I went to the convent and I sort of fell for her. I thought, "Shoo, she's so nice." I lost my appetite at the table. Oh, I didn't know I was in love. We sat at the same table, but we barely looked at each other. We weren't supposed to look at anybody too much that you liked, especially loved. I didn't call it love. I just called it a very nice person, and I liked her and I know she liked me, but she didn't dare look up and look at me. Finally, I was very sick and the head nurse, she said I might be better if I talked to that particular sister, Elizabeth.

We never, we never sneaked. That was the only time I ever talked to her. I said, "I've not come here to be banned. I just came here to find God and somebody to love because I was lonesome and alone." So then she put her arms around me and hugged me a couple of times. I found out that she liked me just as much I did her. She said, "We can't be that way here," and then she kissed me and hugged me.

After that, a priest came up the stairs and said, "We have decided that you will have to leave the convent." I said, "Oh no, she did that. She kissed me. I didn't want to do that." The superior said that I had proved that I was not fit to be a nun. They put me in a room and locked the door. That night they took me out in the dark and put me on a train. I don't know if she is there now. Maybe she died, but anyway, boy, I sure didn't die.

MARDI GRAS KREWES

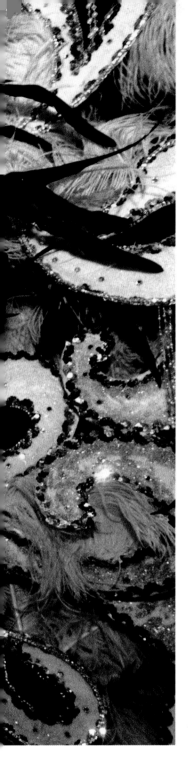

*The feast before the fast, Mardi Gras is the day to indulge in all that will be denied during the forty days of Lent. The Carnival season stretches from January 6, Twelfth Night, to midnight on the eve of Lent. More than seventy parades are held in New Orleans and the surrounding area during the last two weeks of Carnival. But the themed parades, trinkets, beads, and doubloons are only the most visible part of Mardi Gras, for the balls held by clubs called krewes to present their royal court of kings and queens are the height of the New Orleans social season.*

*The oldest krewe, Comus, was founded in 1857. As more krewes were formed, several all-female and all-black krewes were organized. By the 1950s the first all-gay krewe, Yuga, had been formed.*

*Early gay krewe membership was secret, and an invitation to a ball was a prize. Now anyone can buy a ticket for a balcony seat, and the krewes have even allowed limited press coverage. But krewes are still cautious about their membership, pointing to the 1962 raid on a gay ball that cost many their jobs when the names of those arrested were printed in the local paper.*

*Armeinius Ball captain Wally McLaughlin, forty-two, and the members of his krewe work year-round on their themed balls, where they present their king and queen in fantasy costumes. Lords of Leather royalty George Hester, thirty-nine, has spent as much as six thousand dollars on his costume.*

*As participants have attempted to outdo themselves and one another, the costumes have grown more elaborate: Petronius had fireworks spewing forth from its queen's costume; Lords of Leather, whose theme was a twist on* The Wizard of Oz, *had a sixteen-foot swirling mass of lights, miniature houses, and fiber to represent the tornado.*

*These photographs were made at the Armeinius and Lords of Leather balls.*

*Wally:* When the balls started, it being illegal to even sit in a gay bar, it was a way to meet other gays. It was almost like a private community center. That's one of the reasons the gay krewes are dying down. There had been twenty-two or twenty-three gay krewes seven years ago. Now there are four. With the more open attitude, young queens, eighteen-year-olds coming out, don't need the krewes. AIDS has taken a big share of it too.

It started out as a spoof of straight balls. Old-line balls are totally formal; your main ambition is to get through the night without falling asleep.

The Mardi Gras parades are the free show, but the balls are a party for our friends. The costumes have gotten much more extravagant. Before, a big costume was the size of a card table; now it is as big as a Mack truck. The straight balls originally were a tableau: they would take you to Venice, Paris, or Broadway for a night. Their whole ball would be Paris streets, like an extravagant theme party.

I try to have misleading themes. This year, we had our twenty-fifth-anniversary ball. Everybody assumed we'd have a costume for each year; instead, we were the anniversary gifts for anniversary years. We try to outdo ourselves every year. It's that competition within ourselves: you have to do better each year. It's friendly competition between the krewes. It's not vicious. And everyone has their own idea of the perfect costume and presentation.

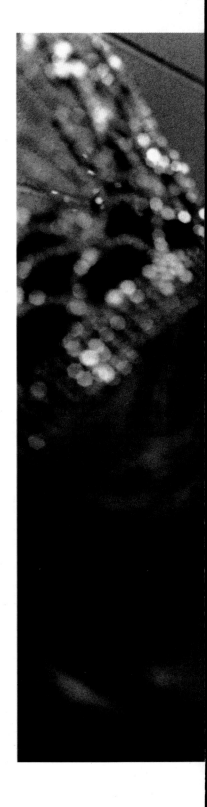

*George:* If the other balls are a satire of the straight krewes, then, if you would, the Lords of Leather is a satire on the gay krewes. It was originally created because other Mardi Gras krewes in town were more oriented to the drag aspect, exactly duplicating the straight Mardi Gras krewes. In the straight Mardi Gras krewes, the queen is the debutante of the year; the king is someone hysterically famous or well-to-do. The debutante season for young ladies coming out, everyone gets presented at a Mardi Gras ball whether it's straight or gay. But at the straight balls, it is a way for the family to present their daughters to society; the queen and all the maids of the court are all debutantes.

We poke a lot of fun at them, naturally. That's part of what makes ours a little more fun to go to than the staid balls where you sit around and watch these guys come out in the exact same costume that they came out in last year. In a gay krewe, you'd never be caught dead in the same costume two years running.

In the gay krewes, the queen is the prime place. Everybody wants to be queen of the krewe. Other krewes were known as a more feminine, female-impersonator-type role, and ours was intended as a way to flaunt feather and fiberboard, and be a man doing it. Though in the last couple of years we've adapted more feathers, and now we've actually been called "the Lords of *Feather.*"

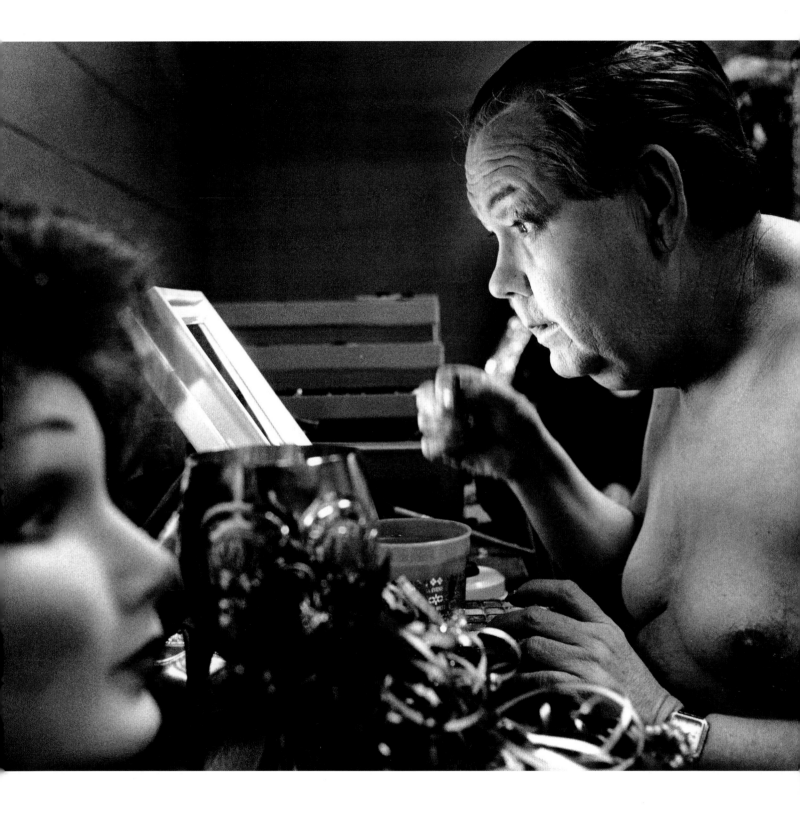

# THE BAND

*Formed in 1982 by seven regional bands, the Lesbian and Gay Bands of America is a federation of twenty-two bands throughout the nation. The organization sent 140 of its members to perform at President Bill Clinton's inauguration.*

*Among the musicians was Patrick Prochaska, thirty-nine, a saxophonist and dentist from Minneapolis.*

*Lynda Chen, forty-four, an alto saxophonist from the Philadelphia Freedom Band, also performed. She teaches singing to elementary school students. Lynda had never played a musical instrument until she joined the group four years ago. She taught herself to play, with the help of band members, who lent her instruments.*

*Ruben Estrada, forty-five, has played with the Pacific Coast Freedom Band in Long Beach, California, for three years. His co-workers at the telephone company helped him raise money to pay for the trip to Washington, D.C.*

*Some members of the saxophone section of the band were photographed after practice on the eve of their 1993 presidential inaugural performance. Ruben is in the center, and Lynda is to the right.*

*Patrick:* I have been with the Lesbian and Gay Bands of America since it started. My own band, the Minnesota Freedom Band, started with Gay Pride in '82. There was a member of our community that played baritone horn, and he just said, "It's really a shame that we don't have a marching band for the Pride Day parade." So he called a few friends, put an ad in the paper. We had some meetings, and we just decided this was a fun thing to do. A lot of us hadn't played our instruments for five or ten years, and it was getting back into music again. It was something that for most of us was probably the highlight of our high school lives. I mean, we were band nerds; there's no two ways about it. It was so fun to be able to do that one thing that really made us feel good and do it again, with other gays and lesbians. It was great. The other thing about it was at that time Minnesota was extremely separatist: lesbians and gay men didn't do anything together. And so that was another big change.

*Lynda:* Everyone needs to belong in some sense, and in this society it's really hard to be accepted by some people, so you want to be in an organization where there are no pretenses. In the band everybody knows that we are either gay or straight and the straight people there are very supportive, everything's very accepting.

*Ruben:* I always felt I was the only gay person in the world. When you get that for so long, it feels good to know that it's not just me. Now, anything that has to do with being gay I want to support and be a part of. The band gives you a sense of community wherever you go. Here, I feel like I am a part of it and I am valued. It makes me feel like I am important.

# SAGERCIZE

*More than a dozen senior citizens gather twice a week for exercise class at the Lesbian and Gay Community Services Center in New York City's Greenwich Village. The class is sponsored by SAGE (Senior Action in a Gay Environment), and is called SAGErcize.*
*The class was photographed during its workout. Near the end of the session, Joe, seventy, stretches under the light.*

*Joe:* When I was growing up gay there was no such thing as a center. Everybody was out on his own, and you had society against you. You might go to a gay bar, but the gay bar might be raided. It's kind of nice now to go to where you don't have to be on guard, where you can relax. It's camaraderie. We're kind of regulars; we stay together.

THE BAY AREA BOXING CLUB

*The Bay Area Boxing Club began when Greg Varney and his lover built a boxing ring in the attic of their home in 1976. The club now meets once a week at a boxing gym in the Mission District of San Francisco.*

*Greg, forty-two, first boxed when he was six. He now is a boxing manager and trainer.*

*Several club members were photographed after a workout. From left to right, they are: Scott McDonald, thirty-seven; Thomas Malott, twenty-seven; Jim Dailey, thirty-six; Bruno Kochis, forty-two; and Dennis Richards, twenty-nine.*

*Scott:* I was told gay men shouldn't box or couldn't box. But I wanted to try it. Some of it is that you build up self-confidence in everyday life. Boxing did that. I'm HIV-positive, and I have been for seven years, and I thought, "If I want to do these things in my life, I better start doing them now." That was a big motivating factor: experiencing things I never had before.

*Bruno:* It's not just violence for violence's sake; it's a male thing to do. It's a release of aggressions. Boxing is a very safe outlet. In this group, you take your lumps, but nobody gets seriously hurt. There's a certain feeling among the members. It's something that happens on a nonverbal level. I don't mean to say that boxing is talking, but in a certain way it's a way of communication. You learn something about somebody when you're boxing them, whether you win or not, whether you can block their punches or you have to take them. There's something revealed about that person. It's nonverbal and it creates a very good feeling between us. It makes us family; it makes us belong.

*Greg:* Boxing is fighting. A lot of gay people, they don't understand it. But that's what it is. It's a fight. Gay people, if they get hit, they tend to go away, or to run, or to use a whistle or something and hope that maybe someone will come. To me, that's not realistic. A whistle's fine if people come, but not everybody comes.

Gay men can fight. And I don't mean box, I mean fight. That's it in a nutshell. You can do anything you want, but until you can stand there and say, "Hey, I'm just good as you, and if you try to push me, I'll knock your lights out"—until you can actually do that, we haven't got it.

# GLORIA DAUPHIN

*Gloria Dauphin was raised in "a kind of June Cleaver family," in Opelousas, Louisiana, the heart of Cajun country. At the age of fifteen, she thought she might be gay and went twenty miles to a university library to read about homosexuality.*

*After graduating from Louisiana Tech University, she returned home, but later moved to New Orleans. Gloria, twenty-nine, has lived in the city since 1988, working in the marketing and advertising departments at a country radio station.*

*Much of Gloria's time is spent as head of a group of lesbians of color. She was photographed after dinner at Dunbar's Creole Cooking, a neighborhood restaurant that she frequents.*

The official name of the group I head is Womyn of Color Unified Lesbian Sisters—"womyn" because we took out the "man." The group started about a year ago with four of us. The way I found out about the group was at the women's bar, Charlene's. On Tuesday they used to have a woman there who cut your hair. I walked in to get a haircut and saw a group of black women, and I never saw any black women there. I just kind of went up and said, "Hey, what's going on?"

They were talking about forming a lesbians-of-color support group. It's kind of gone from there. We usually average about twelve women at our meetings that are twice a month.

I think it is important to develop an identity for people of color who are trying to deal with coming out of the closet. I felt like we were this invisible group that I was sure had to exist, but didn't seem to exist, because you didn't see anyone. There was no place to go, no place to find out, to meet other people. We have made people of color visible in the New Orleans gay and lesbian community.

I've heard comments that some people are kind of uncomfortable about getting involved with the group. They see the organized gay community as white only. One criticism is that they refer to us as a bunch of "wannabes." You know, wannabes are the way blacks might describe other blacks who they see as wanting to be white.

But a lot of our gay role models are not people that look like ourselves. One thing that I used to get very excited about, to see the talk shows and the magazines which seemed always to be writing about gays and lesbians. But after a while I started feeling like there's no one that looks like me. And there's still that something there I can't quite relate to.

*Making its home in an old funeral parlor on Joy Road in Detroit, the Full Truth Unity Fellowship of Christ Church is just three years old. The gay church began as informal meetings in private homes and has grown to 110 members.*

*Renee McCoy, the founding pastor, was raised in the Roman Catholic Church and spent thirteen years as pastor at a gay church in New York before returning to her native Detroit. Renee and Allen Spencer, the assistant pastor and minister of music, both hold full-time jobs in addition to their duties at the church. Renee, forty-two, works as a consultant for the Detroit Health Department, and Allen, thirty-two, is an orderly at a nursing home. Allen, who began preaching at the age of fourteen, was photographed with the choir during a Sunday morning service.*

*Allen:* One Sunday I wanted to try something different. And you can't get any more different than Full Truth. I even remember the suit I wore. I went in a nice little two-piece, it was teal green, a little white shirt, a teal green tie, little green shoes to match, socks, and all looking cute: I just got a fresh haircut.

And I sat there, and they were coming in in blue jeans, sweatpants, and shorts. And then I looked up and here comes Renee in tennis shoes. I said, "Okay, this is Sunday morning worship?" Then one guy came in in a suit, and I thought, "Maybe we can live through this experience today."

I was curious. There were very affirming things on the walls. I remember looking at the board: "You will no longer be called forsaken." And I thought that was so wonderful; it was a confirming experience for me. I thought, "Wow, God hasn't forsaken me just because I am gay."

I kept going back. The message was different than I was used to hearing. They were affirming of my lifestyle, that God has me as a gay man, and as black gay man. God loves me and, yes, I can be accepted as I am. Singing at Full Truth is a wonderful thing. It's confirming to lead the choir, to show them that they are okay to sing God's praises.

*Renee:* In the black community the church is the most powerful institution, and it's always represented civil rights and social services. I felt like there was a need for those kinds of services in the black gay and lesbian community. I had only been meeting people who were broken and bruised, and there was nobody out there who was meeting their needs.

God and religion are so much a part of our culture that no matter what, it all goes back to *what does God say.* We needed something that connected this whole people to our past, to that spirituality. The church was just a good place to do it in. People come to church because they want something. The church is only effective if it works to transform your life. God's love is for everybody. And don't believe the hype. We are children of the same God. As children of the same God, we are all heirs to the same power, the same beauty, the same love. God's love is for everybody.

# KEVIN BYRD

*Kevin Byrd, thirty-three, says he does "as little as possible" to earn a living in Enterprise, Mississippi. Kevin spends much of his time renovating the family plantation home, which had been vacant for twelve years. On the grounds, Kevin maintains enough animals to stock a petting farm: three dogs, five goats, two pot-bellied pigs, six lovebirds, two ponies, and a mule.*
*Kevin also passes his time as the host of a local radio show. He was photographed in his bedroom.*

I am a native of Clarke County. I'm related to half the families here. Everybody's known me my whole life. It's totally different than if someone openly gay came from outside into this little tiny community of roughly three hundred people. An outsider would probably face violence. When our local postmaster came out down here, the little old ladies were wearing white gloves to gather their mail so they wouldn't get AIDS from the mail.

I realized I was gay probably when I was six, but I didn't come out until I was eighteen. I couldn't come out here in Clarke County, so I moved away. I went to the Mississippi Gulf Coast and spent ten years down there.

But I came back home. It's where I belong. My family was here before the Civil War. This house was built slightly before the Civil War. It was a hospital for both sides, passing back and forth several times.

Enterprise was the capital of the Confederacy for one day. Oh yes, one day. They were on the run then. I'm still looking for the gold that they left behind.

I've got a radio show every month on WYKK, 98.9 FM. It's called "The Maverick Hour." Ninety minutes long. It's a political show stressing tolerance. WYKK plays country, but I play everything. I have played *Rocky Horror* on my show. I played the New York City Gay Men's Chorus Christmas album at Christmas. That was a record breaker here. People weren't really ready for that. I am the major sponsor for this, so once a month is about all I can afford. It's the only way I can stay on. It costs $450.

Some churches tried very hard to have me canned. They threatened a boycott of all the advertisers on the station. By paying my own way, I can do what I want. And if I want to play queer music on Sunday night, I can do it.

I've had wide support. You get the occasional redneck that calls in with the Sodom and Gomorrah comments. But in my little town here, I'm still Kevin.

# CHARLES GERVIN

*Charles Gervin, thirty-seven, lives in his native city of Detroit.*
*Charles was photographed at the offices of HOPES (Healing Ourselves through Preven-*
*tion, Education and Services), an HIV risk-reduction program targeted at Detroit's black*
*gay community. He earns his living as project director for HOPES. Foremost, Charles is*
*a poet.*

When people look at my picture in this book, they will see two things. First, they will see whether or not you are a good photographer. That will be on the surface. But below the surface, because it is another human face, what they'll see is reflections of themselves.

I'm sure there are probably lines in my face and what might seem like a certain attitude or an expression that will bring them back to themselves. Perhaps it might enlarge what they think the world is. I think that is the power of pictures—to bring the intimacy of someone far away in terms of time, condition, and attitude very close to us. To challenge us not only to be ourselves but to be beyond ourselves, to open ourselves to this other thing.

To see themselves, that is the only way they can reach me. The self seeing the self is what I hope happens. There are a lot of people who don't like looking at themselves. On many levels it's very painful to regard ourselves in all our beauty and all of our ugliness, too.

People are so divided. I don't mean gays against straights, I mean divided against themselves when it comes to sexuality and emotions. It's not a very comfortable playground. So when you regard somebody and it's an issue of sexuality, it triggers a lot of uncomfortable notions. To look at someone and to find another human being repulsive, the bad feeling comes from the pit of the stomach of the person who's doing the looking, not the person who is looked at. That's the balm—to know that we have nothing to do with their disgust. It's disgust they choose to see us as.

# GEAN HARWOOD AND BRUHS MERO

*Gean Harwood and Bruhs (pronounced Bruce) Mero first kissed on New Year's Eve in 1929. They have been together ever since, for sixty-three years.*

*Gean, eighty-four, worked for Paramount Pictures and later for New York City's building department, retiring from the department in 1971.*

*Bruhs, eighty-two, first worked in advertising and then became a professional dancer, working on and off Broadway. He and Gean wrote songs together and opened the Dance Gallery in New York in 1939. To make ends meet, they lived in the studio where Bruhs taught dance and held original modern-dance performances using music composed by Gean. In 1943, shortly after Bruhs's first solo Broadway appearance, in which Gean accompanied him on the piano, Bruhs suffered a heart attack. His dance career abruptly ended. After a long recovery, he worked as a writer for a trade publication.*

*In the mid-1980s, Bruhs began to show signs of Alzheimer's disease. By 1991, he required around-the-clock supervision and was moved to a nursing home. Gean still lives in the Lower East Side studio apartment the two shared for thirty years.*

*Gean takes an hour's bus ride through the city to the nursing home just four blocks northwest of Central Park. During a visit, Bruhs gives little reaction to Gean. Gean kisses him on the cheek, then, clasping Bruhs's hand, leads him to the recreation room.*

*There a lone woman sits inches away from a loud television. Gean begins to play the piano, battling the sound of the TV. The piano wins, and gradually patients and staff drift in to listen to Gean. One woman sings, while another requests show tunes. Bruhs sits in a chair by Gean's side. Gradually he begins to tap his foot to the music and even smile. Gean plays songs the two composed, periodically smiling at Bruhs. But Bruhs's vacant stare does not return the warmth. He does not utter a word, let alone sing any of the more than thirty songs he wrote with Gean.*

*The two were photographed as Gean said good-bye to Bruhs in his room at the nursing home.*

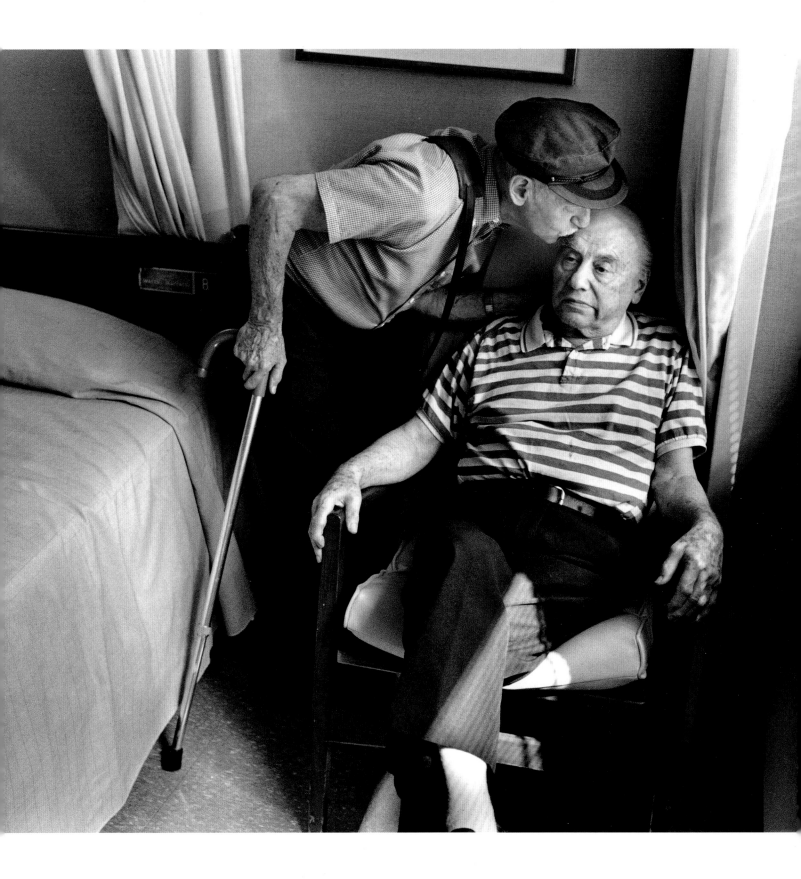

*Gean:* Very frequently, gay people meet in bars or on a park bench or something, but our meeting was very legitimate. We were introduced by mutual friends. It was near the end of 1929.

I was very attracted to him but I was warned that even though he was circulating in some gay company, he was very seriously committed to a young woman. They were actually engaged, and so I decided I should really cool it and not indicate my feelings. Then a very dramatic thing happened with my apartment.

The landlord found out that one of my roommates was gay. He knocked on the door and said, "I want you all out of here within forty-eight hours." So I said, "We have a lease." He said, "Well, your lease is canceled; I am not renting any of my apartments to fags."

So this was my first brush with discrimination, and I was twenty years old. I called Bruhs, because I was new in town and I didn't know many other people. And he needed a place then also. That's how we started living together.

I was very, very much attracted to him, but I had declared him off-limits because of his arrangement with the girl. I didn't want to do anything to interfere with that, but we finally became much closer.

It must have been fate that threw us together. Bruhs didn't have a date that New Year's and neither did I. Our building was full of musicians, and they used to have wonderful parties. They had a big one on New Year's Eve, and we were both invited.

We went and had quite a little bit to drink. After the thing was all over we went back upstairs together, and I guess the liquor and all had reduced the inhibitions we both felt. That was really the first time that we came together. The chemistry was right, and it just went on from there and developed. There didn't seem to be any recriminations on Bruhs's part. He seemed to be very content that this was really what he wanted, that he had really found himself. I think he was very reluctant to commit to anyone, and it wasn't until he met me and spent some time with me, living under the same roof, that he got to feel that this was something that he could commit to. He finally broke off the engagement with the girl and decided to stay with me.

We lived very closeted lives, and I was never out to my family. But after all, with two men who never married and had been together all these years, they had to realize that something was going on. This wasn't a "normal" arrangement. Bruhs finally came out to his family around 1979. I thought to myself afterwards, "How silly. How silly I have been all these years to be hiding. We have nothing to be ashamed of."

I feel very grateful that we did share all those wonderful years. During the Depression in '33, Bruhs lost his job here, so he worked with his brother temporarily in Florida. He was very lonely there. He finally wrote a poem about it. I thought it was the basis for a song, and when he sent me a copy of it, I set it to music. This was our very first song. It's called "Come and Take My Hand."

The songs were a joint creation for us. Sometimes Bruhs wrote the words first and I put music to it. Sometimes I had to change the meter a little bit, but not enough to detract from the poem. Other times, I composed something in the way of music and he put words to it. Sometimes it required sitting side by side and doing the thing.

We wrote our last song together in 1982. The title was "I'll Never Say Good-bye." I couldn't play that for the longest time. It was too hard, remembering Bruhs how he used to be. When I had Bruhs at home, I made a point to play one hour a day because that's how we could communicate. When he sang he was himself. At one time he knew all the words, he could do them by heart. Then we used sheets. Now he doesn't sing at all.

The last few months that I spent with Bruhs were so, so tremendously tense. I was actually very insecure. I felt my own safety was being threatened because he was so unbalanced. Even though I was totally reluctant about giving up on him and putting him in an institution, it finally got to the point where this was a twenty-four-hour ordeal for me.

Some of the people at the nursing home understand that we were life partners, but not everyone does. I go to visit, but it isn't very rewarding for either one of us at this stage of the game. Bruhs vaguely recognizes the fact that I am somebody he should know, but he's not able to sort it out—who I am and why I am there.

There is a certain amount of frustration on his part. In the early days when he was there, he used to say to me, "There's something wrong here. What is wrong?" He was very troubled for a long time. Now he doesn't say any of those things anymore. He would take hold of my hand and say, "I only want to be with you." That was hard on me, and now the indifference he has is equally difficult for me to handle. I guess there's no way out of that; it is the nature of the disease. With Alzheimer's, in some ways it's more difficult for the person giving the care than the one receiving it.

The relationship was something that meant a great deal to both of us. We really felt that we belonged together. There were times in our existence when there were some very strong pulls away from each other, but there was a continuity there that neither one of us could ignore, and somehow we seemed to be destined to be together.

It's very hard to put into words what that span of time really meant. I find it at this stage practically impossible to describe.

# NOTES & ACKNOWLEDGMENTS

Though gay men and lesbians can be found anywhere, it's quite another thing to find those who are willing to be photographed by a *Washington Post* photographer doing a book. All names and places in the book are factual, with one exception: as noted in the introduction to their section, fictional first names were used for Laurel, Margaret, Peter, and Avery. Any slight anonymity given to other subjects was accomplished solely through the deletion of facts.

Interviews ranged in length from thirty minutes to several days. The text is edited, though the voice of the speakers remains intact. Factual aspects of the subject, such as age, are correct for the date the photograph was made, freezing this information in time, just as the picture has done with the subject's appearance. All subjects are named from left to right as they appear in the photograph unless otherwise noted. The pictures were made in 1993, with the following exceptions: Trussell, Kigin, and Trussell (1989); the Prom Queen (1991); the Birthday Party, Rainey Cheeks, Mary Courtland, Joseph Dittfeld, Greg Greeley, Ray Hagen, Hunt and Harner, Susan Hester, Frank Kameny, Avery's Family, Dale McCormick, the Rodeo (in part), and Dan Stevens (1992).

I now understand why so many authors dedicate their books to their families. Authors knowingly choose the all-consuming task, but their families are forced to live with the decision without ever having had a vote in the matter.

This book is dedicated to my mother, who always chooses to support her children simply because they are her children. My father and sister as well as the rest of my family were also of great help. My partner, Marileen Maher, helped in every aspect of the book. I cannot thank her enough.

This book would not have been done without the generous support I received from *The Washington Post*. I am indebted to Joe Elbert and Michel duCille. I also thank Leonard Downie, Robert Kaiser, and Tom Wilkinson for their support.

Even though this book bears only my name as its author, I had invaluable help from dozens of friends and colleagues. Many thanks to all of you: the editors, Kathryn Jourdan, Mary-Ellen Phelps, Kara Swisher, and Elizabeth Chang; the picture editor, Michel duCille, and, for their varied opinions, Bob Herne, Christoph Walker, John McDonnell, Carol Guzy, and others; and the photography assistant/intern, Tyler Mallory.

Also many thanks to other *Post* colleagues who helped: Dan Murano, Chris White, Vanessa Barnes-Hillian, Gerald Martineau, Craig Herndon, Dudley Brooks, Keith Jenkins, Dayna Smith, Juana Arias, Ray Lustig, Frank Johnston, Robert Reeder, Elana Winsberg, and Debra Gertler.

Thanks to other journalists for their help: Robert Baker, Fred Sweets of the *Los Angeles Times*, Paul Bartels of the New Orleans *Times-Picayune*, Sylvain Metz, Gary Kaupman at the *Southern Voice*, Phillip O'Jibway of *Cruise* magazine, Nancy Boutillier of the *Bay Area Reporter*, Jeff Ofstedahl of *Echo*, and Valda Lewis of *Just for the Record*.

Thanks to transcribers Lynn Ward, Olwen Price, Kerry Topel, and Rose Gershon.

Many people and their organizations helped me along the way, and I give my heartfelt thanks to them. They include Wilton Tenney, Susan Nadeau, Nan Stone, Deirdre Maher, Linda Bourquin, Mimi McGurl, Ellen Spiro, Pam Hall, Anita Hall, Scott Rafshoon, Ellen Rafshoon, Phillip Jourdan, Sharon Jourdan, Jodi Hines, Candy Bell, Judy Portock, Dan Iversen, Michael Lentz, Atlantic States Gay Rodeo Association, Arizona Gay Rodeo Association and the Tucson Satellite Chapter, Mark Miller, Bill Darnell, Bill Conn, Fred Molina, George Hester, David Stranger, Lords of Leather Mystic Mardi Gras Krewe, Krewe of Armeinius, Wally McLaughlin, Uncle Bert's Place, Bill Flint, Kudzu Konnection, Lambda Youth & Family Empowerment, Laurie Bell, Dan Goldstein, Senior Action in a Gay Environment, Michael Thompson, Harvis Weekly, Lambda Chai, Charlene Schneider, Rip Naquin, Jim Bailey, Daniel Troppy, Art Rietveld, Vonceil Smith, Karen Lowens, Cecilia Marchetti, Asians and Friends of Atlanta, Bootsie Abelson, Kay Crutcher, Bob Bernstein, Bobbi Bernstein, Teena Blakeney, Renee Reno, Kathy Switzer, Sue Dabbs, Gretchen Brewer, Lesbian Life Drawing, Lyn Duff, Metropolitan Community Church of San Francisco, Linda Brown, Nancy Pollock, Gay and Lesbian Parents of Marin County, Ken Grantham, Trevor Hailey, Ron King, Jean Podrasky, Jyotsna Sreenivasan, Vanessa Moore, Dino Duazo, Steve Takemura, Gay Asian Pacific Alliance, Charles Hopkins, Barbara Wood, Penny Rich, Margy Lesher, Su Penn, Lesbian Connection, Jerrie Linder, Minor Miracles Softball Team, Jeanne Re Montandon, Donald Rafal, Eddie Sandifer, Phyllis Christopher, Rob Shields, Rose Gladney, Tricia Walker, Amy Lindsey, Amanda Coupland, Lisa Snider, William Waybourn, Gay and Lesbian Victory Fund, Human Rights Campaign Fund, National Gay and Lesbian Task Force, Black Gay and Lesbian Leadership Forum, Robert Bray, Bill Walker, Gay and Lesbian Historical Society of Northern California, District of Columbia Coalition of Black Lesbians, Gay Men and Bisexuals, Willie Weiss, Ginny Mills, James Mills, Heidi Leiter, Missy Peters, Gladys Paige, Julie Dobo, Nadia Malley, Jane

Winer, Carol Galbraith, Jay Allen, Camille Carroll, Prince William Gay and Lesbian Alliance, Detroit Women's Coffee House, Gary Patch, Chris Rush, Craig Snow, Greg Varney, Brendan Daly, Peter Covar, Gail Ross, Valerie Warner, Lee Morris, Judy McMoran, Morgan Dodd, the Bickersons, Ken Ashton, Patricia Cooper, Ross Howell, Zoon Nguyen, Michael Bento, and Full Truth Unity Fellowship of Christ Church.

Much of my research was done through several years of reading the many newspapers, magazines, and journals serving the lesbian and gay community, such as *The Washington Blade, Bay Area Reporter, The San Francisco Bay Times, Outlines, The Advocate, Southern Voice, The Houston Voice,* and *Lesbian Connection.*

A special thanks to The Virginia Museum of Fine Arts Fellowship Foundation for a 1993–94 fellowship. A big thanks to The Corcoran School of Art, The Corcoran Gallery of Art, Philip Brookman, and Samuel Hoi for making the exhibition of these photographs possible.

Many thanks to Eric Marcus for his eloquent foreword and for introducing me to Harper San Francisco. And thanks to my fine editors at Harper, Barbara Moulton, Lisa Bach, Carl Walesa, and Rosana Francescato, designer Jaime Robles, and others at Harper Collins, Matthew Lore, Mary Peelen, Jonathan Mills, Cathy Quealy, Ellen Georgiou, and Michele Wetherbee.

And finally, a special thanks to all who agreed to be interviewed for the book. It took all of you and more to create this book, and I thank you.